CECIL SHERMAN

FORMATIONS COMMENTARY

VOLUME 3

MATTHEW–MARK

Smyth & Helwys Publishing, Inc.
6316 Peake Road
Macon, Georgia 31210-3960
1-800-747-3016
©2006 by Smyth & Helwys Publishing
All rights reserved.
Printed in the United States of America.

The paper used in this publication meets the minimum requirements of
American National Standard for Information Sciences—
Permanence of Paper for Printed Library Materials.
ANSI Z39.48–1984. (alk. paper)

Library of Congress Cataloging-in-Publication Data

Sherman, Cecil E.
Cecil Sherman formations commentary / by Cecil Sherman.
p. cm. — (Cecil Sherman formations commentary series)
ISBN 1-57312-476-1 (pbk. : alk. paper)
— ISBN 1-57312-477-X (pbk. : alk. paper)
— ISBN 1-57312-478-8 (pbk. : alk. paper)
— ISBN 1-57312-479-6 (pbk. : alk. paper)
— ISBN 1-57312-480-X (pbk. : alk. paper)
1. Bible--Commentaries.
I. Title.
II. Series.
BS491.3.S44 2006
220.7--dc22

2006012289

Table of Contents

A Word from
the Publisher

On most any Sunday, in thousands of Bible study classes across America, one common question is asked in the midst of discussing that day's session: "What does Cecil Sherman say about this passage?"

Cecil Sherman has served as the primary commentary writer for the *Formations* series of adult Bible study for nearly fifteen years. Across these years, he has offered insight through nearly 700 sessions across 45 issues of the commentary and addressed an extensive amount of Scripture. His work with *Formations* has made him a fixture in many Sunday school classes.

Formations began publication in the summer of 1991. At that time, the series offered a teaching guide and a learner's guide. That fall, a commentary was added to the line. For the next four quarters, the writing for the *Formations* commentary was shared by a varied collection of writers in each issue. While readers welcomed the addition of the commentary, we heard a persistent call for a regular ongoing writer.

In September 1992, Cecil Sherman was introduced as the new writer for the *Formations* commentary. At that time he was serving as the charter coordinator of the Atlanta-based Cooperative Baptist Fellowship, itself only a few years old. In spite of a heavy travel schedule and numerous administrative responsibilities, Sherman made a priority of writing. When he retired from the CBF in 1996, he made it clear that he gained great satisfaction in writing the *Formations* commentary and wanted to continue providing this popular resource.

Many Sunday school curriculums offer a commentary as a way of balancing the heavily structured writing of the other books in a series. The teaching guide offers teachers needed guidance in leading group studies, while the learner's guide provides a base of content that helps adults approach and better understand what is happening in a given Bible passage.

Both the teaching guide and learner's guide are strongly engineered resources, since writers are given detailed direction and their resulting work is carefully edited to help the session hold a focus and fit properly within the unit.

The commentary writer is given a great deal of freedom in how the chosen passage is approached. Good commentaries provide useful background information and help the reader more fully dig into the Scripture. A good commentary also reveals the personality and character of the author in ways that help us remember that interpretation is ultimately an intimate and personal activity.

Beverly Crowe Tipton, who served as editor of *Formations* for eight years, said of her experience working with Cecil Sherman, "It was my privilege to 'read behind' Dr. Sherman for eight years. With each manuscript he submitted, I learned to expect that he would provide a volume of insightful study directed toward Bible teachers. Dr. Sherman knows the Bible, the church, and even better, he knows how to tell a story. His commentaries provide a depth of biblical scholarship that he brings to life through rich storytelling based on a lifetime of experience and spiritual wisdom. His ability to communicate the gospel in a way that balances bold proclamation with good pastoral sense is a rare gift of ministry to a thirsty church and its people that he loves so much."

Cecil Sherman's commentary writing is notable not only in the way he interprets Scripture, but in his ability to draw readers into a dialogue around a passage. Cecil has a gift for taking passages that might otherwise seem complex and distant and helping us discover them as rich and engaging. He approaches the Bible as a good friend, expecting each encounter with the text to deepen our relationship with and understanding of Scripture. Cecil's commentary both invites us to share in his conversation with Scripture and models for us a solid approach for biblical interpretation. It is easy to read his commentary and feel almost like we are sitting with him on the front porch, sharing a pitcher of sweet tea and discussing life, the Bible, and faith. It's a wonderful way to read the Bible.

It is tempting to point to Cecil's warm style of writing and interpretation as his core asset. However, such an approach would ignore the fact that he is also a solid Bible scholar. His writing is clearly informed by careful research into biblical languages, backgrounds, theology, and archaeology. Cecil holds a Master's in Theology from Princeton Theological Seminary and a Doctor of Theology from Southwestern Baptist Theological Seminary. Even in his retirement, Dr. Sherman continues periodically to teach courses at the Baptist Theological Seminary of Richmond.

Cecil Sherman is also an experienced churchman. He knows the waters of the local church extremely well and uses that experience to offer seasoned guidance to matters that inevitably arise in the life of congregations. Part of his insight was earned through decades of ministry service in active and vital churches, including pastorates at First Baptist Church of Asheville and Broadway Baptist Church in Ft. Worth. Sherman's love of the church bleeds through each and every commentary he writes, speaking to the real issues and challenges congregations face.

Cecil's first editor was Mark McElroy, now senior editor for Smyth & Helwys. Mark sums up the enormous contribution made by Cecil's commentaries: "Cecil Sherman's *Formations* commentary has always been a labor of love on Cecil's part—love for the Bible and love for those who endeavor to shape themselves according to the truth of Scripture. Cecil always respected the reader in a way that was epitome of grace. In spite of his enormous pedigree and the depth of his experience, Cecil wrote each week as if he was required to earn again the right to be heard. Cecil's commentary has been a gift. And, like the gospel truth to which it pointed, it is a gift that keeps giving."

These five volumes that make up the *Cecil Sherman Formations Commentary* collect the uncommon wisdom, insight, and wit that Cecil's readers have come to treasure week after week through the years. When we realized the amount of commentary that Cecil has created over these years, it was an easy decision to preserve the commentary in book form, making it available to students of Scripture now and across the years ahead.

We are honored to share the gift of Cecil Sherman's insight with you in this series of commentaries. May they inspire in us a lifelong love of Scripture and of learning.

David Cassady
Executive Vice President & Publisher
Smyth & Helwys Publishing

History Is Not Meaningless

Matthew 1:1-17

ORIGINALLY PUBLISHED JULY 18, 2004

Introduction

When I saw our text, I thought my editor had made a mistake. Could I really be expected to write a commentary on a genealogy? With some frequency the Bible has a long list of unpronounceable names; those are the parts we skip. And now a lesson from a genealogy! I was amazed but not amused. How in the world can I find meaning in these verses? Even more daunting, how can I put enough salsa on this text to make it tasty? Then I began to read about genealogies in the Bible, and the subject became a little clearer.

Early Hebrews did not attach importance to genealogies: "Early Hebrew family records (Ex 35:30) reach only to the 'third and fourth generations' (Ex 20:5). As late as the Persian period, only once in the Jewish Aramaic papyri does identification of a witness reach the fourth generation" (*The Interpreter's Dictionary of the Bible*, E–J [New York: Abingdon Press, 1962], 363). But that changed.

After captivity, Ezra and Nehemiah put great store on Jewish purity. Jews had been scattered after the fall of Jerusalem (587 BC). Priests were required to prove they were Jews and that they were not soiled by intermarriage with Gentiles. With the requirement for "proof" of purity came other reasons for genealogies:

• individual identity for legal purposes—like inheritance
• nobility had to establish their "rights"
• demonstration of relationship to important events or people

What puts us off and makes for hard reading actually attracted Jews of the first century. If I were setting out to write a "life of Jesus," I would not begin as Matthew did. But Barclay put it this way: "It might seem a daunting proceeding to present the reader right at the very beginning of his book with a long list of names to wade through. But to a Jew this was the most natural, and the most interesting, and indeed the most essential way to begin the story of any man's life" (*The Gospel of Matthew*, vol. 1 [Philadelphia: Westminster Press, 1958], 1).

I majored in history in college; I teach history and am biased about it. I think history is undervalued in our educational programs. Some of my intelligent students are unlearned about church history; they hardly know the rudiments of American history. My family doesn't know or care about genealogy. I can name my grandparents only to the fourth generation. Evidently they held Henry Ford's opinion of history. In July 1919, Ford brought a libel suit against the Chicago *Tribune*. He was asked about history and made a remark that has become famous. Ford said, "History is bunk." Jews didn't think so, and their genealogies bear witness to a sense of who they came from, who they were, and where they were going. We need to know what the genealogy of Jesus meant to the Jews who read it, and we need to see if it has meaning for us.

I. The Genealogy of Jesus Connects.

Jesus was a Jew. To Matthew's audience, this idea had powerful appeal. Jews knew their history. To be descended from Abraham meant you were a Jew. To be descended from Abraham through David meant your pedigree was tip-top. There are forty-one generations cited, but "the rabbis would have regarded Abraham and David as the high points in the genealogy" (Sherman E. Johnson, *The Interpreter's Bible*, vol. 7 [New York: Abingdon Press, 1951], 251).

The sense of the genealogy was to "connect" Jesus to important people in Jewish history and to "connect" Jesus to Jewish expectations. The Messiah was expected to come from the line of David, and Matthew tells us Jesus was.

The idea that Jesus was of David means little to me, so when I see it in the New Testament, I take no notice of it. However, David's relationship to Jesus is a theme in the New Testament.

• At Pentecost, Peter said, "Fellow Israelites, I say to you confidently, of our ancestor David that he both died and was buried. He knew that God had sworn that he would put one of his descendants on his throne" (Acts 2:29-30). Peter was connecting Jesus to David and to the destiny God had in mind for the Jews.

• Paul's letter to the Romans begins, "Paul, a servant of Jesus Christ, called to be an apostle, set apart for the gospel of God, which he promised beforehand through his prophets in the holy Scriptures, the gospel concerning his Son, who was descended from David according to the flesh" (Rom 1:1-3). Note the connection to David.

• The New Testament closes with a vision of John: "It is I, Jesus, who sent my angel to you with this testimony for the churches. I am the root and the descendant of David, the bright morning star" (Rev 22:16).

• Matthew does not leave the "son of David" connection to genealogy. He repeats it. Crowds were amazed at Christ's ability to heal and exclaimed, "Can this be the Son of David?" (12:23b). A Canaanite woman shouted at Jesus, "Have mercy on me, Lord, Son of David; my daughter is tormented" (15:22). Two blind men at Jericho shouted, "Lord, have mercy on us, Son of David!" (20:29-30). Near the end, as Jesus entered Jerusalem for the last time, the crowds "went ahead of him shouting, 'Hosanna to the Son of David!' " (21:9).

Jesus was connected to people who had the highest standing in Jewish life; he was qualified to be the Messiah. That's the point Matthew set out to make.

II. The Genealogy of Jesus Interprets.

Frank Stagg sees in the genealogy an interpretation of the history of the Jews:

> The overriding concern of the genealogy is to trace the fortunes of God's people from the great expectations of Abraham to the seeming fulfillment in David (vv. 2-6), then the decline from David to the Babylonian exile, where all seemed to be lost (vv. 7-11), and finally from the hopelessness of the Babylonian exile to the true goal in Jesus Christ (vv. 12-16). (*The Broadman Bible Commentary*, vol. 8 [Nashville: Broadman Press, 1969], 81)

William Barclay sees the same thing. In a section he titles "The Three Stages," Barclay says the genealogy is arranged in three stages:

(1) Verses 2-6a tell of the generations from Jesse, father of David. This part "takes the story up to the rise of Israel's greatest king" (*The Gospel of Matthew*, vol. 1, 3).

(2) Verses 6b-11 tell a story of decline: "And Josiah the father of Jechoniah and his brothers, at the time of the deportation to Babylon" (1:11).

(3) Verses 12-16 end like this: "And Jacob the father of Joseph the husband of Mary, of whom Jesus was born, who is called Messiah" (1:16). Abraham was given a promise of glory for Israel. It appeared King David fulfilled the promise; that appearance was dashed in Babylon. Jesus came to restore Jewish destiny.

There is a hopefulness that runs deep in the Bible. God is making sense of the maze and the confusion that is life. The story of humankind is going toward end time, judgment, and eternity. All sorts of interpreters of history are around us. Cynics hold that history moves toward oblivion. Christians see the hand of God in it. Sometimes we can make no sense of it. In those dark times a Christian holds tight to faith. "We know that all things work together for good for those who love God, who are called according to his purpose" (Rom 8:28) is still in the Bible. Matthew was telling his first readers (and us) that God is in history and will make sense of it.

III. The Genealogy of Jesus Includes.

The first point went to some length to point out the "connections" of Jesus. To get the attention of a Jewish audience, Matthew could not have cited better credentials. However, the genealogy includes more than heroes. Note the types in this most interesting list of names.

(1) There were four women. This was unusual: "Remarkable is the inclusion of four women (Tamar, Rahab, Ruth, and the wife of Uriah). Customarily, Jewish genealogies give only the names of men" (Stagg, *The Broadman Bible Commentary*, vol. 8, 81). It is remarkable that women were in the genealogy; it is more remarkable when you consider who they were. Rahab was a harlot of Jericho. Ruth was a Gentile. Tamar was no saint; pretending she was a harlot, she tricked her father-in-law into getting her pregnant with twin sons. Bathsheba (Uriah's wife) committed adultery with David. So although Jesus came of Abraham and King David, there were parts of his background much like yours and mine.

(2) Kings other than David are mentioned—Hezekiah, Manasseh, and Josiah. Hezekiah and Josiah were "the good kings." The sacred writers

describe Manasseh as wicked; he led Israel into idolatry. There is no white-washing in the list.

(3) Then there are ordinary people. Some of the names listed appear no other place in the Bible. Abraham Lincoln's line fits: "God must like ordinary people; he made so many of them." Most of the people in the genealogy were "just folks." (It should be noted that this genealogy is not complete. All commentators note that there are not enough names to stretch across the years. Stagg says, "His purpose is to relate Jesus to David and Abraham, not to give a literal and complete genealogical catalog" [ibid.].) Spliced in among the great were plain people. Jesus was born to a plain young woman, Mary. Joseph was a carpenter. Just folks.

(4) The genealogy of Jesus implies the Holy Spirit: "And Jacob the father of Joseph the husband of Mary, of whom Jesus was born, who is called the Messiah" (1:16). George Buttrick said, "No human birth, however royal, can account for Jesus; he came by the direct and creative act of God. There is a mystery in Christ which human factors alone cannot explain" (*The Interpreter's Bible*, vol. 7, 252).

A child of Joseph and Mary, even if descended from Abraham and King David, could not do what Jesus did. The source for Jesus has to go back to God.

IV. The Genealogy of Jesus Looks Forward.

Our text reads, "An account of the genealogy of Jesus the Messiah, the son of David, the son of Abraham" (1:1). The word for "genealogy" in the New Revised Standard Version can be translated several different ways. Here is how other translations have rendered this verse:

• The King James Version—"The book of the generation of Jesus Christ"
• The Revised Standard Version—"The book of the genealogy of Jesus Christ"
• J. B. Phillips—"This is the record of the ancestry of Jesus Christ"
• The New English Bible—"A table of the descent of Jesus Christ"

All these versions struggle with Matthew's word "genesis" (the same word that names the first book in the Old Testament). Literally, the word means "beginnings." In Jesus, God is picking up the pieces of a sad history, pushing them to the side, and starting over again. Jesus is a fresh start for God and therefore for us.

The idea of starting over again appears often in the Bible. Sometimes it seems God is not so much starting over as moving forward: "Long ago God spoke to our ancestors in many and various ways by the prophets, but in these last days he has spoken to us by a Son, whom he appointed heir of all things" (Heb 1:1). God was raising the bar in revelation. In Jesus we could see more of what God was like and what God wanted of us.

Life is like this genealogy. It moves forward and upward. Even death is not final. God is not finished with us. God has more in mind. Always, God is working with a future tense. If God is looking forward, we ought to be looking forward too.

I found more in "the genealogy" than I expected. Most important is the subtle, hopeful interpretation of history in it. History is not meaningless. God is in it. That is a faith statement: "In Christ God was reconciling the world to himself" (2 Cor 5:19). That's what Matthew tells us in the genealogy.

When Kingdoms Collide

Matthew 2:13-23

ORIGINALLY PUBLISHED DECEMBER 27, 1998

Introduction

Most church people think they know everything there is to know about "the Christmas story." Compared to other parts of the Bible, most church people probably do know more about the Christmas stories than they know about the Hebrews' deliverance from Egypt or Paul's journeys. Still, there are bits and pieces to "the Christmas story" that are slightly known. Today's text is material that we don't talk about much.

Telling this story will be more important than usual because it is a difficult text. Matthew was writing to Jewish Christians, making a case for Jesus' having been the promised Messiah. What Matthew was trying to tell his first readers is not easy for us to hear. The way he used the Old Testament is puzzling to us. These are only some of the difficult issues in this lesson.

I. The Story.

Matthew's account of Jesus' birth is very different from Luke's. To "get into" Matthew, it would be wise not to read Luke at all because it is so easy to combine the two accounts to make a blended nativity. We do better when we let Matthew tell his story without concern for how well it "fits" Luke. The same would apply to Luke. Matthew's sequence is as follows:

(1) The genealogy of Jesus is from Abraham to Joseph (1:1-16).

(2) Joseph is told of the unusual circumstances surrounding Mary's pregnancy (1:18-25). Mary is hardly mentioned. Joseph is the principal parent in Matthew's account. Joseph named Jesus, and in Matthew that was critical.

(3) Wise Men come " 'from the East…' asking, 'Where is the child who has been born king of the Jews?' " (1:1-2). Note that Jesus is recognized by Gentiles.

(4) Joseph, Mary, and the baby Jesus are in Bethlehem. In another dream, God warns Joseph to "take the child and his mother, and flee to Egypt, and remain there until I tell you" (2:13-15). Joseph acts promptly. Like many other Jews, the family escapes Herod and finds refuge in Egypt.

(5) Herod the Great was cruel. The Romans trusted him, and he served the Romans faithfully. It would be hard to overstate his capacity for raw meanness. William Barclay illustrated Herod's murdering ways with this sad litany:

> He murdered his wife Marianne and her mother Alexandra. His eldest son, Antipater, and two other sons, Alexander and Aristobulus, were assassinated by him. Augustus, the Roman Emperor, had said bitterly that it was safer to be Herod's pig than Herod's son. (Barclay, *The Gospel of Matthew*, vol. 1 [Philadelphia: Westminster Press, 1958], 20)

So, if Wise Men from the East said Jesus might rival Herod as "king of the Jews," then the baby boy must be killed. But God warned and Joseph obeyed. The infant Jesus was saved.

(6) Herod's fear of a rival had to find outlet. He calculated how to kill Jesus and determined that every male child in Bethlehem had to die. By this method, he could not miss killing the newborn "king of the Jews." This led to "the murder of the innocents" (2:16-18). Some commentators believe this is not a historical event, that it didn't really happen, because Matthew's Gospel is the only account of it. It was, however, in character for Herod.

(7) Because of Joseph's alert obedience, Mary and Jesus are safe in Egypt.

(8) Finally, Herod the Great dies. At his death, God spoke a third time to Joseph in a dream. "Get up, take the child and his mother, and go to the land of Israel, for those who were seeking the child's life are dead" (2:20). Always obedient to God's voice, Joseph went back to Israel.

(9) Joseph was prudent. Archelaus, son of Herod the Great, was the new ruler over Judea. Like his father, he was unpredictable and often murderous. Joseph did not go back to Judea. Instead, yet another dream led him to Nazareth (2:22).

This outlines the first two chapters of Matthew. When chapter three opens, nearly thirty years have passed.

II. Peculiarities in the Story.

Peculiarities in this case mean that there are unusual ways Matthew tells about Jesus. We need to take note of these peculiarities:

(1) Joseph has four dreams from God.
- An angel tells him to take Mary as his wife. Do not be afraid. Her child is of the Holy Spirit (1:20-21).
- An angel tells Joseph to flee with Mary and the baby to Egypt (2:13).
- When Herod died, "an angel of the Lord" told Joseph to take the family back to Israel (2:19).
- "Being warned in a dream," Joseph settled in Galilee instead of Judea (2:22).

Dreams appear often in the Bible. Jacob, Joseph, Daniel, and Paul either had dreams or could interpret them. There may be more to dreams than our generation is willing to admit. God has used them in the past.

(2) Joseph and Mary never speak a word in Matthew's birth narrative. A narrator tells the story. Mary is as much a bit player in Matthew's Gospel as Joseph is a bit player in Luke's, but neither speaks in Matthew. God is the mover, speaker, planner, and preserver. God initiates all action in Matthew.

(3) Matthew does not give details. How long were Joseph, Mary, and Jesus in Bethlehem? How long did they stay in Egypt? Where did they go in Egypt? We are not told.

(4) Matthew's use of Scripture is puzzling. He uses Old Testament passages to buttress his story.
- Matthew never drops a Scripture from Mark or any other source. There are at least sixty-one in his Gospel.
- Matthew is not trying to persuade "outsiders" Jesus is the Messiah; he is writing for insiders. "The conviction that Jesus is the Christ is the presupposition of his use of Scripture" (*The New Interpreter's Bible*, vol. 8 [Nashville: Abingdon Press, 1995], 153).
- By our standards, Matthew is careless with his Old Testament quotations. Often they seem to have little connection with what he is illustrating. But by first-century Jewish standards, Matthew's use of Scripture is not only acceptable, it is extraordinarily effective.

III. An Interpretation of the Story.

The lesson title, "When Kingdoms Collide," seems a stretch for the text, but Matthew wrote with a world view in mind. Understanding Matthew's perspective helps us grasp the power in this lesson.

(1) Jesus always moved on a world stage. From birth, this babe born in Bethlehem was destined for greatness. Herod, a person of enormous consequence, noticed and feared the birth of Jesus.

Wise Men came "from the East." They were Gentiles. Jesus and the gospel he preached was not meant for Jews alone. Jesus would make his mark among Gentiles.

Jonah is one Old Testament illustration that the gospel was for the world. But that gospel was suppressed, and a near hatred for Gentiles became Judaism's public face. Jesus would change that.

(2) Jesus has always threatened a "Herod" kind of mind. Throughout history there have been too many Herods—cruel people who do murder and meanness as habit. People who are hard and cruel always recognize Jesus as their natural enemy. They are hard; he was merciful and forgiving. They are jealous; he was self-emptying and given to service. They want more; Jesus gave more. They excluded; Jesus included. They think of the present; Jesus kept eternity in view. They set themselves up as gods; Jesus was of the very nature of God. And he wanted the commitment and loyalty only God can ask.

Jesus did not let this side of his nature go without comment. Jesus warned his followers that discipleship would be hazardous duty. "Blessed are you when people revile you and persecute you..." (Mt 5:11). So when Herod murdered innocent children to try to kill Jesus, it was only the first of a pattern. Jesus prompts strong feelings.

(3) Jesus has always been preserved to God's purposes. Joseph didn't save Jesus from Herod. God did. Joseph obeyed God, and obedience is Joseph's virtue. God stepped in, gave a plan to rescue, and would not allow the mission of Jesus to be cut short. Matthew saw the big picture; and in the big picture was the hand of God preserving, protecting, extending Jesus to his mission.

Much of my preaching has been done from a small vantage point. I looked so intently at my text (usually just a few verses) until I lost the big picture. Matthew never did. He saw the whole picture. God sent Jesus to save. God would not let Herod or Pilate, Pharisees or Judas, popes or denominations, self-seeking preachers or unlearned teachers keep Jesus from his assigned task. Through all these people and roadblocks God has moved to enlarge and preserve Jesus and the people who bear his name. I think

Matthew had a vision of a world-wide Church. He saw the spread of the gospel. His Gospel is written with an eye to a Christ who would overpower and rise above a Caesar. It was unthinkable in his time. From our perspective it doesn't seem strange at all. Caesar is still studied; Jesus is worshiped.

When you see what Matthew was doing, our title doesn't seem out-of-touch at all. Kingdoms have collided and they still do. A Kingdom of peace still wrestles against the kingdoms of this world. A Kingdom of fairness still wrestles against all kingdoms of greed. Just like Matthew said it would be.

When Good News Is Bad News

Matthew 3:1-12

ORIGINALLY PUBLISHED DECEMBER 12, 2004

Introduction

In Jesus' day, the priesthood was in the hands of the family of Annas. Over an extended time, the priesthood had declined. Once they were the custodians of high ideals; now they were functionaries involved in a temple routine. The glory was gone from their work, and some priests were corrupt. In fact, the "chief priests" (see Jn 11:47) led the way in plotting to kill Jesus. Their mission was to maintain the religious establishment in Jerusalem; the lofty ideals of the prophets were gone.

Pharisees never numbered more than six thousand, but their influence went well beyond their numbers. They held themselves up as the truly dedicated ones. They committed themselves to keeping the law of Moses, but their actions mocked it. Under the pretense of keeping the law, they tried to imagine every situation that could occur on the Sabbath and to determine which were permissible. Petty rules replaced Sinai rules. Throughout the Gospels, we have record of the Pharisees pestering Jesus about rules. Finally, Jesus had enough. You can find his exasperated response in Matthew 23.

Priests who had lost sight of their high and holy mission and a group of "super Jews"—the Pharisees—crippled the religion of ordinary people. They did not stop believing, but they had little enthusiasm for faith.

Almost hidden inside Judaism was another group who did not make headlines. I refer to Zechariah and Elizabeth, Joseph and Mary, Simeon and Anna. Sometimes theologians call them "the remnant." These remnant people held fast to the highest ideals of Moses and the prophets, and they were always alert to any sign of the promised Messiah.

It was hard to be part of "the remnant." God had not spoken in more than four hundred years. That's how long it had been since the last of the Old Testament prophets. When Jesus was born, most people had no idea that God was doing "something new." Simeon and Anna were exceptions. They detected God's new plan. God had another way to get the attention of the masses—a man called John the Baptist.

I. God Broke the Silence, 3:1-6.

Many preachers are tame, with an agenda more personal and ambitious than God-driven. Occasionally, there comes a different kind of preacher. He's not afraid of making prominent people angry. She's not politically correct. This kind of preacher speaks truth so plainly that ordinary people perk up.

John the Baptist was that kind of preacher. He was not looking for a bigger church. He didn't even attempt to draw a crowd. He was a recluse living in the Judean desert. His personal habits were eccentric. We would call him "a character."

John spoke for God. Just months older than Jesus, John was about thirty years old when he moved onto the public stage. In the life span of the ancient world, John was in his prime. He boasted no academic pedigree. He honed his mind and message in a lonely place. He had sought God's thoughts, and they became his. He was different from the rabbis, the Pharisees, and the priests.

I imagine Jews of 2000 years ago had about as much cynicism as we do. They were not easily impressed, but John got their attention. It had been so long since a real prophet had spoken that people argued whether or not God would ever speak again. However, when John began to preach, ears that had grown deaf to all things religious listened.

The Judean wilderness is forbidding country. It can be hot and windy. Water is scarce. That's where John began to preach. That anyone even knew he was on the earth is a minor miracle, but the word got around. A different kind of man, one who sounded like Amos, Micah, or Jeremiah, was out in the desert. I can hear the word on the street in Jerusalem: "You've got to go hear this fellow. He tells the truth no matter what." The crowds came because God broke the silence. They didn't go to the Jordan to hear John. They went to the Jordan to hear a prophet speak for God. Ordinary people recognized that long silent Voice.

II. God's Clear Voice, 3:5-10.

Three powerful ideas came out of John's preaching:

(1) Repent. "Then the people of Jerusalem and all Judea were going out to him, and all the region along the Jordan, and they were baptized by him in the river Jordan, confessing their sins" (3:5-6). Preaching about repentance is not popular these days. We consider the Ten Commandments optional, but we take seriously "Thou shalt not judge." If you preach "Thou shalt not judge," you buy a little space for your own sins. Scripture supports this view, but it is not a subterfuge for license.

John was not troubled by convention nor was he politically correct. People still gave lip service to the law of Moses, but for years they had cheated on the law. John the Baptist didn't slap their hand and send them home. He gave them a powerful symbol. He dipped them in the Jordan River; the dipping was a sign that they were washed clean of old sins and were making a fresh start. This was not the first time baptism was used in Judaism. When Gentiles converted to Judaism, they were baptized.

Did John's baptism wash people's sins away? No. Christian baptism is an outward sign of an inward change. For centuries churches have asked people to make public their religious resolves. Therefore, baptismal confessions serve a useful purpose...as they did in John's day.

George Buttrick defined repentance: "The word 'repent' implies a radical change of mind. It looks to the past in honesty and remorse, and then in a right about-face it looks to the future in resolve on a new way of life" (*The Interpreter's Bible*, vol. 7 [New York: Abingdon Press, 1951], 263). G. F. Moore went a step further. He said, "Repentance is the sole, but inexorable, condition of God's forgiveness and the restoration of His favour, and the divine forgiveness and favour are never refused to genuine repentance" (quoted in William Barclay, *The Gospel of Matthew*, vol. 1 [Philadelphia: Westminster Press, 1958], 44). Moore was right. Repentance is not an addendum to the Christian religion; it is at the center. We can't get close to God until first we have repented our sins. It was not just John the Baptist saying, "Repent." It was God saying what God has always been saying to wayward children.

(2) Being kin to Abraham will not get you to heaven. "Do not presume to say to yourselves, 'We have Abraham as our ancestor'; for I tell you, God is able from these stones to raise up children to Abraham" (3:9). Some thought that because they were kin to Abraham, they were automatically saved. Having Christian parents will not save me any more than having Abraham for a distant relative would save a Jew.

(3) Luke tells us more about the message of John than Matthew does. Luke records this exchange between the crowd and John: "And the crowds asked him, 'What then should we do?' In reply he said to them, 'Whoever has two coats must share with anyone who has none; and whoever has food must do likewise' " (Lk 3:10-11). In a practical way, John asked people to care and then share. Good religion sensitizes the nerve endings of the soul. Bad religion can rationalize away such sensitivity; good religion always heightens it. The effect of John's revival was social. This element in John's preaching was in the prophets, in Jesus, and in the early church. Repentance proceeds to good deeds.

III. God's Intention Is Recognized, 3:11-12.

"I baptize you with water for repentance, but one who is more powerful than I is coming after me; I am not worthy to carry his sandals. He will baptize you with the holy Spirit and fire" (3:11). John the Baptist did three things in his preaching:

- He clearly identified sin.
- He used a symbol (baptism) that caught popular imagination. To be baptized was to confess sin and repent of it.
- He never thought he was the "main event." He always looked beyond himself to Another.

John's humility was unusual: "One who is more powerful than I is coming." Luke gives more detail about the birth of John the Baptist than the other Gospels. An angel appeared to Zechariah, John's father, saying, "Do not be afraid, Zechariah, for your prayer has been heard. Your wife Elizabeth will bear you a son, and you will name him John. You will have joy and gladness, and many will rejoice at his birth, for he will be great in the sight of the Lord. He must never drink wine or strong drink; even before his birth he will be filled with the Holy Spirit. He will turn many of the people of Israel to the Lord their God. With the spirit and power of Elijah he will go before him, to turn the hearts of parents to their children, and the disobedient to the wisdom of the righteous, to *make ready a people prepared for the Lord*" (Lk 1:13-17, emphasis mine).

Popular theology theorized that Elijah would return from the dead to prepare the way for the Messiah. John dressed, ate, and sounded like Elijah. He smoothed the road for the Messiah. He identified Jesus. John's Gospel tells us more about the way Jesus was identified: "The next day he saw Jesus coming toward him and declared, 'Here is the Lamb of God who takes away the sin of the world!' This is he of whom I said, 'After me comes a man who ranks ahead of me because he was before me' " (Jn 1:29-30).

John knew his place in God's design. John was the last of the Old Testament prophets; he was the first to introduce the central figure in the Christian religion. John was pointing to something new.

One last idea is in the text. "His winnowing fork is in his hand, and he will clear his threshing floor and will gather his wheat into the granary; but the chaff he will burn with unquenchable fire" (3:12). John predicted that Jesus' presence would force a decision. We have to decide what to do with Jesus. He pushes us to claim or reject him. A "winnowing fork" divides, separates. This session ends with an awesome question: What will you do with Jesus?

Responding to Temptation

Matthew 4:1-11

ORIGINALLY PUBLISHED FEBRUARY 28, 1993

Introduction

The temptation of Jesus is hard material. If we get it right about what the temptations meant to Jesus, we can still make bad interpretation when we begin to say what the temptation of Jesus means to us. So, reach for all the help you can get on this material. And God willing, I will give you some thoughts you can use.

I. Background Can Help.

Three ideas may help unlock this text. Let me give a brief comment on them; they are not the lesson. They are the setting for the lesson.

(1) *Sequence.* All three synoptics (Matthew, Mark and Luke) place the temptation of Jesus immediately after his baptism. In Mark baptism and temptation are blended into one paragraph (Mk 1:9-13). Both baptism and temptation are a part of one event: the introduction of Jesus. In the baptism Jesus was identified "voice from heaven" that said, "This is my own dear Son, with whom I am pleased" (Mt 3:17 TEV). But the same God who identified Jesus also would test him before ministry. Think of both baptism and temptation as part of Jesus' initiation into public service.

(2) *Wilderness.* If you go east from Jerusalem you descend to the Jordan River. The Judean landscape is severe; it is tough, dry, usually very hot. Almost no one lives in "the wilderness." So, to go from John the Baptizer's revival into the wilderness was a short journey, and it was certain Jesus meant to be alone.

Note the text says, "the Spirit led Jesus into the desert…" (4:1 TEV). He was not enticed to temptation; he was led by the Spirit of God. Ponder two other Bible giants who spent time alone before great service. Moses would spend forty years in the silence of desert, and it was out of his desert time God spoke (see Ex 3). Lost to most of us is the desert time of Paul. In Galatians there is this autobiographical comment, "And when he decided to reveal his Son to me, so that I might preach the Good News about: him to the Gentiles, I did not go to anyone for advice, nor did I go to Jerusalem to see those who were apostles before me. Instead, I went at once to Arabia…" (Gal 1:16-17 TEV). And remember the prophets. Often they refined their God insights with time in a desert place.

Moderns who walk around with radios and have to be with people all the time are missing more than they know. Sometime everyone has to have alone time. We will never know just when Jesus realized who he was and what his mission was. But whatever the process was by which that revelation came, baptism and temptation had to be key elements in his own self-discovery. This insight came when he was alone.

My brother-in-law was a casual Christian. All his life he had gone to church, but the spark was missing. One weekend he took a chance on a Lutheran retreat. In this retreat my brother-in-law was asked to go off by himself and remain silent for an extended period of time. During the silence and isolation God shouted at him, and he became an extraordinarily dedicated disciple of Jesus. The transformation did not come from preaching or from the company of any group; the change came in the silence and the aloneness. He found himself and was found of God.

(3) *Temptation/Testing*. Think of temptation as testing. God does not tempt us, but God does test us. Barclay says it well: "Temptation is not the penalty of being a man, temptation is the glory of being a man" (William Barclay, *The Gospel of Matthew*, vol. 1 [Philadelphia: Westminster Press, 1958], 56). I suspect most of want a path free of steep places and a life spared temptation and hard testing. But I am not sure that is to our good. James put it this way, "My brothers, consider yourselves fortunate when all kinds of trials come your way, for you know that when your faith succeeds in facing such trials, the result is the ability to endure" (Ja 1:2-3 TEV). If Jesus had to be tested before service, should we expect less?

II. What Did It Mean? What Does It Mean?

We need not worry. Most of the temptations that came to Jesus will never come to us, because we are not Jesus. His special powers and special identity made for special testing. It should be a point of concern that we are not tested more than we are. Only great Christians face great testing. But whether we be spiritual pygmies or apostles, all who follow Jesus will have some testing. So, what did the tests mean to Jesus? What do they; mean to us?

(1) *Turn stones into bread, (4:2-4).* I wonder if Jesus knew he had miraculous powers. There is no record he had yet used such power. Now Jesus was very hungry, and it was in his power to feed himself by turning stones into bread. But if he had, he would have bent divine power to meet his hunger. At a later time, when he hung on the cross there came this taunt, "He saved others, but he cannot save himself" (Mt 27:42 TEV). Jesus was very careful about how he used his powers.

Note that at a later time Jesus would feed people with his capacity to do a miracle. But he would not turn his ministry to feeding alone. In John 6 there is the full story of the feeding of the five thousand. And then the crowds followed Jesus all the more. And when they found him, Jesus said, "You are looking for me because you ate the bread and had all you wanted.... Do not work for food that spoils; instead, work for the food that lasts for eternal life" (Jn 6:26-27 TEV).

This insight about feeding people to get a crowd was with Jesus from the beginning. He closed the first of the tests with this word: "Man cannot live on bread alone, but needs every word that God speaks" (Mt 5:4 TEV). So, Jesus aimed his ministry at the spiritual needs of people more than at the physical needs. But be careful how this is taught. Either/or is treacherous.

(2) *Sensationalism, (4:5-6).* One of the ways to get inside what was happening in the "testings" is to go back and study the Jewish expectations for the Messiah. He was to appear suddenly, in striking fashion (see Mt 3:1). And the Messiah would be protected by the angels (see Ps 90:11-12). Were Jesus to make some sensational entry into the Temple, he would certainly meet Jewish expectations and get an immediate following. Jesus rejected sensation as a means to get a crowd. If Jesus rejected sensation, ought we not reject showmanship in religion today? Hollywood and Nashville styles have been baptized and brought to church, but the people we get that way will go away when the entertainment goes. Jesus would have none of it—neither should we.

When I was a boy, I sometimes helped my brother "throw his paper route." One early morning I was folding The Fort Worth *Star Telegram*, and I noticed a strange headline: "Seminarians Hurt in Fall." I read the article. Two students at Southwestern Seminary had jumped from a high place on a building. Both had broken both legs. Both said they expected God to catch them and spare them the injury that would normally come to anyone who jumps from a high place. They thought God would intervene; God did not. They were hurt quite badly. They had rather foolishly "put the Lord…God to the test" (Mt 5:7 TEV). God had not failed them; they had failed to use the common sense God has given all reasonable people. We are to take some chances for God. We are not to put aside prudence and good sense.

(3) *"Let's Make a Deal," (4:8-10).* I suspect this was the temptation that was the hardest to sort through. If Jesus would just "make a deal" with the Devil, his ministry would have been altogether different. The "testing" put it this way. The Devil took Jesus to a place where he could see "all the kingdoms of the world," and then came the proposition: "All this I will give to you," the Devil said, "if you kneel down and worship me" (Mt 4:8-9 TEV). If Jesus would not be the constant enemy/ opponent of the Devil, the Devil might find some way to get along with Jesus. It would have changed the Gospels and compromised everything.

A little religion is no threat to the devil. A serious disciple has to be faced by the devil. Jesus did his entire ministry straight; he cut no deals. This "test" is faced by you and me when we are spiritually sensitive enough to, know we are facing it. We are most like Jesus when we are the devil's enemy; we are least like Jesus when we find some way to "have it both ways."

Conclusion

The text ends with a tantalizing word: "Then the Devil left Jesus…" (Mt 4:11a TEV). This thought comes to mind: Was this the end of temptation for Jesus? Had he whipped the Devil once and for all? Not at all. Jesus was like us. The Garden of Gethsemane is evidence that Jesus was not through with hard testing (see Mt 26:36-46).

Putting First Things First

Matthew 5:17-26

ORIGINALLY PUBLISHED FEBRUARY 14, 1993

Introduction

Matthew was the most orderly of all the Gospel writers. It was his style to pull together the several teachings of Jesus on a common theme, package them tightly and present them to us. Three illustrations come to mind:

(1) The Sermon on the Mount is a compressed statement of many teachings of Jesus. He could have spoken all these ideas in a single sermon; I think he spoke these ideas over the whole of his ministry and Matthew compressed them into what we call The Sermon on the Mount.

(2) An extended passage on witnessing is in Matthew 9:35–10:42. If you want a primer on how to act when you go forth to speak for Jesus, Matthew has a guidebook for you.

(3) Then notice how Matthew pulls the parables into one section of his Gospel. Matthew 13 is one parable after another. But the systematic mind of Matthew gave us a parables section of his Gospel.

Now if Matthew was orderly in the way he presented the life of Jesus to us, how much more orderly ought I to be as I present this comment to you. Today's text comes in three paragraphs. All the parts are very important; so I would suggest you try to give a measured amount of time to each. If you skip and dart on this lesson, you will leave unsaid basic teaching. So, get it right and get it tight. To help you organize what you say I offer these suggestions:

I. The "You Are" Passages, 5:13-16.

Jesus is getting ready to reinterpret the Law. The reinterpretation will be profound. But the power of the Christian movement would not rest on the profundity of the theology of the interpreter (Jesus). Rather, the Christian movement is measured by the changed lives of the disciples. This is the basic idea in the first teaching. So, "You are like salt for all mankind" (Mt 5:13 TEV). Again, "You are like light for the whole world" (Mt 5:14 TEV).

Now you see why I called this the "You Are" section. Here is the big idea in this passage: Jesus came to give a clearer statement of what God expects of us than any previous teacher. We are the followers of Jesus. If we do not model the teachings...and we model the teachings by

- being like salty salt; we are a small presence that changes the taste of the whole meal.
- being like a bright light on a tall pole; we are out for all to see the product of the teachings of Jesus.

Some people are gaudy and ostentatious in their religion, and Jesus had a word for those people (see Mt 6:1-18). We are not to do our praying, our giving or our fasting to be seen of people. But the warning about ostentation does not retract the plain statement of today's text. Finding the right touch is hard. "Hot dog" religion, "show-off" piety is offensive. But Jesus could not have been talking about these excesses. He was looking for some examples, and that is where people like you and me come forward. We are examples of the product.

So, who are the Christians? What will I be like if I become one? Do I have to be like some strange people I've known who say they are "good Christians?" These are some of the questions in the minds of people who are looking at Jesus and wondering about following him. Jesus is telling us we are examples of the "finished product." "You are like salt for all mankind...You are like light for the whole world." If that be so, we have to get it right. We have to learn what Jesus taught correctly and model it faithfully. This is the first teaching in today's lesson.

II. A General Statement About the Law, 5:17-20.

I suspect this paragraph would have prompted more comment among the Scribes and Pharisees than any other section of The Sermon on the Mount. The Law (the first five books of the Old Testament, sometimes called The Torah) were the constitution and Bill of Rights and the Bible all combined to a good Jew. The Law was sacred far more than our secular, irreverent generation will ever understand. So, when Jesus began to talk about the Law, he had their attention. In this section some basic guidelines are laid out:

(1) Jesus says he has not come to "do away" with the Law (5:17a TEV). That would have evoked a sigh of relief from his audience. But what they did not know was that the reinterpretation Jesus would give the Law would be so radical until some would declare he was, in fact, "doing away" just the same. Keep this in mind when you read about the intense debates between Jesus and the Pharisees. He was "messing" with the Law. He was touching what was too sacred to be touched. But at the outset Jesus says, I'm not going to do away with the Law.

(2) Jesus said, "I have come...to make their teachings come true" (5:17b TEV). And here Jesus is doing what the Messiah was predicted to do. He will explain and make clear the teachings of the Law.

(3) Jesus said obeying the Law was a measure of greatness in the Kingdom (5:19). There is none of the "just do what feels good." The Christian religion is orderly, and in Christ is lined out for us.

(4) Jesus said we could enter the Kingdom of God only if our faithfulness to the Law was greater than the faithfulness of the Pharisees (5:20). And this must have taken his hearer aback. No one was more serious about keeping the Law than the Pharisees. So, this will take some explaining.

Now let me depart the immediate text and get into the sense of Jesus. Think about his ministry. He told people it was not of first importance that they keep Sabbath law; it was more important that they be compassionate to hurting people (Mt 12:1-14). But keeping the Sabbath was a part of the Law. He told his disciples to go ahead and eat; fasting could wait until a later time (see Mt 9:14-15). But the Law tells us to fast. And then on other occasions Jesus forgot about washing just so before eating even though the Law spoke of washing rules. And on and on this kind of illustration could run. Sometimes Jesus put aside some of the Law. And then at a later time the Church would lay aside all the sacrificial Law, for we believe Jesus was the last and final sacrifice for all time. So, all at once Jesus honored the Law and he laid a pretty heavy hand on the Law. What are we to make of this? Here are some ideas you may want to consider...

(1) Jesus put aside petty Law. And Jesus was the one who decided what was petty and what was not. This would include washing, Sabbath rule, fasting.

(2) Jesus reinterpreted basic Law. Matthew 5:21-48 are illustrations of the way Jesus laid hands on the Law and lifted the Law to a higher power.

(3) Jesus affirmed eternal Law. Some parts of the Law are for all time. Jesus gave us that Law. We are to love each other. We are to forgive each other as God in Christ has forgiven us. We are to be compassionate. We are to be hopeful that God will come and redeem all that is broken, fallen. We are to work for the coming of the rule of God in the kingdoms of people. This is eternal Law. Jesus powerfully underlined it and gave it permanence.

I have written the above paragraph to help the thoughtful teacher who is wondering: Seems to me sometimes Jesus honored the Law and sometimes he set it aside. The rules I've given may make some sense of what appears capricious in the way Jesus handled the Law.

III. An Illustration of the Way Jesus Reinterpreted the Law, 5:21-26.

Jesus reached back into the Ten Commandments and chose Exodus 20:13; "Do not commit murder: anyone who does will be brought to trial" (Mt 5:21 TEV). This would be his first illustration of the way he would reinterpret the Law. He leaves the words in place, but he gives them a twist, a different meaning, a deeper application. And watch the way he does this so forthrightly; he is not sneaky or clever at all. "You have heard that people were told in the past…. But now I tell you…" (Mt 5:21a and 5:22a TEV). And this same pattern will be repeated in the other reinterpretations (see 5:27, 31, 33, 38 and 43). In each instance he boldly contrasts Moses with himself. "You have heard it said…but I tell you…."

And there is more pattern in Jesus than just the words he used. In each instance of reinterpretation Jesus gives the Law a deeper, inner application. Not many people are going to wince at the Exodus commandment, "Do not commit murder" (Ex 20:13 TEV). So, the teaching is abstract. And I dismiss the teaching by saying, "That teaching does not apply to me; I've never done murder." That is the way I think. I have to think most of the people in class are acting/thinking as I am. If the Law will just stay as Moses stated it, I am home free. This is one part of the Bible I've honored, and I am a good boy.

Jesus internalizes the Law. He seems to be arguing that the reason we kill is because we hate and because we have enemies. So, the Law is restated, "But now I tell you: whoever is angry with his brother…" (Mt 5:22 TEV). Of a sudden I am in the lesson. I know some people who have "done me wrong." And I am packing that anger around in my mind/heart. And until I loose that anger through the Bible process of forgiveness, I am breaking the Law of Jesus. Not many people are murderers, and at church on a Sunday morning the number of murderers is exceedingly small. So, the Law of Moses does not have anything to say to us good folks. Then Jesus comes with another inter-pretation, and being good becomes much, much more complex.

The application goes on to tell us to "make peace with your brother" before we try to do worship (Mt 5:24 TEV). This is a part of the text we pass over to our hurt. I suspect more worship is "cart before the horse" at this point than any other. We can't worship God until we get right with the brother/sister. Jesus said before we even try to worship we need to "get right" with each other. Churches are family. Ties are close. Sometimes we live together in church for decades. We gather slights and hurts, wounds and grudges. These keep us from worship. And they destroy us when we try to be salt and light.

This lesson has plenty to say to us all. Teach all the parts, for one part is tied to the previous part. The parts are built one on top the other. And God bless you as you open the Bible. It is a high work you do.

How to Pray

Matthew 6:1-8

ORIGINALLY PUBLISHED NOVEMBER 16, 1997

Introduction

When I was a little boy, my parents took me to the Polytechnic Baptist Church on the southeast side of Fort Worth, Texas. Sometimes our pastor, Dr. Baker James Cauthen, would ask Brother Gibson, a retired preacher in the church, to lead in prayer. When that happened, I gave up going home any time soon. Sunday lunch would have to wait. When Brother Gibson prayed, he went on and on. I believe the man prayed for ten minutes or more. One time Dr. Cauthen interrupted him to say, "Brother Gibson, let's bring this to a close." I have no memory of anything the man said in his prayers. All I remember was the interminable length of Brother Gibson's public prayers.

Jesus lived in a time when being pious was counted a virtue in Jewish society. Some Jews called attention to themselves when they observed their religion. It was against the background of this public display of piety that Jesus gave some instructions about how we ought to do religion. He addressed three disciplines: giving alms, praying, and fasting.

Not many people fast as a part of their religious disciplines, but nearly all Christians give money to the Lord's work and also try to pray. This lesson is directed toward prayer.

I. Pray in Private, 6:1-3, 5-6.

Jesus said, "Beware of practicing your piety before others in order to be seen by them" (6:1a). He used illustrations from Jewish life to prove his point.

Pharisees would call attention to themselves when they gave money, so Jesus said, "Whenever you give alms, do not sound a trumpet before you" (6:2). He said almost the same thing about people who make public prayers. They would "stand and pray in the synagogues and at the street corners, so that they may be seen by others" (6:5).

Public prayer is an exceedingly treacherous act. In spite of my best efforts, I have a hard time forgetting that I am speaking before an audience. My intent is to speak to God; all prayers are supposed to be directed heavenward. But my humanity takes over, and before I know it, I am preaching to the audience instead of praying to God. This does not mean public prayers should be excluded from worship. It does mean to *watch out.*

A story has made the rounds for thirty years. I hope it is true, for it makes my point. Bill Moyers was serving in Lyndon Johnson's administration. At a government luncheon Moyers was asked to "say the blessing." In a quiet voice Moyers began to pray. From the other end of the room Johnson interrupted the prayer to say, "Speak up, Bill. We can't hear you." Moyers raised his voice and replied, "I was not speaking to you, Mr. President." That says it all. Bill Moyers had not forgotten to whom public prayers are supposed to be directed.

There are things to be said in real prayer that do not lend themselves to a public meeting. The confession of my sin is done best in private. The plea for direction in the tight places in life is best left to private prayer. Intercession for a hurting friend can hardly be done in anything but private prayer.

So, Jesus said, "Whenever you pray, go into your room and shut the door and pray to your Father who is in secret" (6:6a). The sense of this text is that God will become a dearest friend, a confidant. We will share our innermost thoughts. All the pain and the joy, the fear and timidity will come out. What we really are will come out. None of the pretense will be in the mix. Only private prayers offer this intimacy and honesty.

II. Pray Simply, Briefly, 6:7-8.

Again, Jesus reacted to the long, wordy prayers of the Jews who made it a point to call attention to themselves in their piety. Like the dear brother I referred to from my childhood, they prayed long, tedious prayers. They left no missionary unprayed for, no good cause unaddressed, no suffering saint unmentioned. This is good and appropriate, but not in public prayer. Do all of the above. Pray for the missionaries. Pray for every good cause. Pray for hurting people. But do it in private. Then how ought we to pray? Let me offer some suggestions.

Pray briefly. Jesus gave us the Lord's Prayer as an illustration of the right way to pray. Notice how tight, compact, and short it is. You can say all the Lord's Prayer in a minute. If that's the way Jesus taught his disciples to pray, then that's the way we should pray.

Pray simply. Jesus told a story about how we should act when we pray. "Two men went up to the Temple to pray: one a Pharisee and the other a tax collector" (Lk 18:10). The Pharisee told God what a good fellow he was. The poor tax collector simply said, "God, be merciful to me, a sinner" (18:13b). That's all, no more. Then Jesus evaluated the worship experience of the two men. "This man [the tax collector] went down to his home justified rather than the other [the Pharisee]" (18:14a). He didn't have to pray a long prayer. The condition of humility and contrition before God was the part that commended the tax collector. The words were not the nut of it; the condition of the heart was. Prayers are not meant to be long; they are meant to be wholly sincere.

Built into the text is an explanation for why many words are not necessary when we pray. "Your Father knows what you need before you ask him" (Mt 6:8b). Some have concluded that if God knows our needs before we ask, why does God not grant our wishes before we speak them? I don't know, but I do know that we are instructed to pray. God is not impressed with many words or clever phrases. God is looking for a right spirit, a good attitude, a dab of humility, and an open mind.

III. Pray for Basics, 6:9-13.

The Lord's Prayer is a model of praying for the basics.

(1) *Reverence God:* "Our Father in heaven, hallowed be your name" (6:9b). Beginning some 600 years ago, people like you and me began to change the way we think. The mind of the Middle Ages was humility. God was in the center, the focus. People were around the edges of the tapestry of life. But slowly with the coming of all things modern, we came to see ourselves as in control and in the center of life. This is flattering. In many ways the genius of people like you and me have revolutionized life. In travel, communications, and daily convenience, modern life is easier than it once was. But are human beings in control? We acknowledge that God is to be "hallowed" and reverenced and worshiped. There is a Power beyond ourselves. This is basic to prayer. People who don't believe it don't pray voluntarily.

(2) *Ask for food:* "Give us this day our daily bread" (6:11). But honestly, most of us assume necessities; we pray for our wants instead of our needs. But once life was lived at another level. In January 1994, I visited Cooperative Baptist Fellowship missionaries in Albania. I had never really been in a country where people lived "from hand to mouth." Farming in Albania is not done for profit. Farming is done to have enough to eat. There are few "cash crops." All crops go from the earth to the table. Seed has to be saved for next spring's planting. Foolish people eat their seed. Wise people hold on to their seed even if it means going hungry in "the starving time," which is late winter and spring, after last year's crop is gone and before next year's crop can produce. Those people would pray for daily bread with a different frame of mind. If we can't see our need of "daily bread," at least we can help someone else get bread. (About 25 percent of the world's people don't have enough to eat.) We can be God's agents to bring bread.

(3) *Ask for and give forgiveness:* "Forgive us our debts, as we also have forgiven our debtors" (6:12). Life gathers all kinds of trash. Disappointments, frustrations, failures, hurts, broken dreams: these are the things that accumulate inside us. If we do not empty the trash, we soon will be a garbage bin of pain and anger. But when we worship as we ought and when we pray as Jesus instructed, we will get rid of that old stuff. We will be hopeful people. We do this when we ask God to forgive us. We do this when we do for others what we ask God to do for us. We can't have more forgiveness than we are willing to give. Forgiveness is basic. It is one of the building blocks of all worship and prayer.

Building a Firm Foundation

Matthew 7:24-29

ORIGINALLY PUBLISHED JUNE 15, 2003

Introduction

Joseph was a carpenter. Jesus was reared as Joseph's son. From his earliest memory Jesus watched as Joseph worked. At first glance, the work of a carpenter seems straightforward enough. A piece of wood, a saw, a hammer and nails. There's not much to ponder in those simple tools. But Jesus saw in the carpenter's work a thoughtfulness that does not meet the eye.

These experiences from childhood were in his mind when he told the story that concluded the Sermon on the Mount. "Everyone then who hears these words of mine" (7:24a) refers to the Sermon on the Mount. Take the time to read Matthew 5–7. It is all at once idealistic and practical, insightful and human. Jesus raised the bar. The basic law of Moses was reinterpreted: "You have heard that it was said to those of ancient times, 'You shall not murder'…. But I say to you that if you are angry with a brother or sister" (Mt 5:21-22a). Jesus took the rules Moses had given and had the nerve to lay hands on them and make them a matter of intention and not just "an act." I've committed no murder, but I've often been angry. With Jesus, religion became more than a set of rules to keep; it became an interior thing, a state of mind. Not killing is not a problem for most; not being angry is nearly impossible.

Let's make one point clear: Jesus is talking about building a life. George Buttrick said, "Every thought is like a piece of timber in our house of life, every habit like a beam, every imagination like a window, well or badly placed; and they all gather in some kind of unity, seemly or grotesque" (*The*

Letters of John and Jude, vol. 7 [New York: Abingdon Press, 1951], 334). So what does the parable about the wise and foolish man mean?

I. The Words of Jesus Are a Foundation for Life.

"Everyone then who hears these words of mine and acts on them will be like a wise man" (7:24). There are two ways to mess up a life:

• I can refuse to think about or examine values, ideas, options.
• I can profess that I live by the words of Jesus but not act on them.

How do people decide how they are going to live their lives?

(1) A few people examine the sayings and ministry of Jesus and decide against following him. They deliberately, thoughtfully choose another way. This is an examined life, but it is not the Jesus way. These people may opt for another religion, or they choose some form of modern paganism.

(2) Most people take the easy way. They don't think about the words of Jesus or anyone else. They "go along" with the whims of pop culture. This parable teaches that just "going along" can get you in big trouble. The "foolish man" didn't think before he built. Prudence and forethought are in the story.

(3) There is the Jesus way of looking at and doing life. Steeped in Judaism. Stated and modeled by Jesus—refined by the apostles and fathers of the church. Reflected on by Christian scholars and priests, pastors and laity…it is the Jesus way.

The starting place for the Jesus way is the Bible. Most of our people have tried to read the Bible, but it is hard to understand. Efforts to read the Bible usually lead to failure and frustration. Here are some suggestions.

• Begin with Mark's Gospel. It is short and clear. Read it three or four times. Read two chapters a day.
• Now read Matthew 5–7 once a day for a week.
• Then read Luke's Gospel. Read it several times, two chapters a day. Stay with it until you get the sense of it.
• Go to the book of Acts. Follow the same pattern.
• Move to Philippians. It is short, happy, and filled with wisdom and the spirit of Jesus.
• Do not attempt Romans, Hebrews, Galatians, and Revelation until you know "the words" of Jesus.

I've used this way of getting into the Bible several times, and most people have found it helpful. It introduces you to "the words" of Jesus. Of course there is more in the Bible, but we need to start with Jesus, then advance to the reflections of wise people on Jesus. In the words of Jesus there is a foundation for life. The witness of the saints and the church is this: Those rock-solid ideas will support and sustain a life.

II. The Words of Jesus Are the Way We Do Life.

"Everyone then who hears these words of mine and acts on them will be like a wise man who built his house on rock" (7:24). The verses that come just before our text are a warning: "Not everyone who says to me, 'Lord, Lord,' will enter the kingdom of heaven, but only the one who does the will of my Father in heaven" (7:21).

There is a half-truth in our church tradition that does us harm. It has a Bible base. When the Philippian jailer was shaken by an earthquake and saw his prison doors open wide, he "was about to kill himself" (Acts 16:27). In his distraught condition he asked Paul and Silas what he must do to be saved. They said, "Believe on the Lord Jesus, and you will be saved, you and your household" (Acts 16:31). That's Scripture, and I believe it. But is this any way to package the words of Jesus under normal conditions? I don't think so. It is a piece of the truth, but after we believe in Jesus we have to learn and obey the words of Jesus.

Jesus wants more than "belief." He wants us to hear what he said and then do what he instructed. That's what "hears these words and acts on them" means. Why don't people "act" on the words of Jesus?

(1) They are unreasonably idealistic. Here are some of the teachings in the Sermon on the Mount:
- "If anyone strikes you on the right cheek, turn the other also" (Mt 5:39).
- "But I say to you that everyone who looks at a woman with lust has already committed adultery with her in his heart" (5:28). When Jimmy Carter said he "had committed adultery in his heart," the press tried to make him look like a fool.

(2) The church has blended the teachings of Jesus, the laws of Moses, and the Wisdom literature of the Old Testament and come up with something more than Moses and less than Jesus. We are establishment, not radical.

(3) The church has been so intent on gathering people that we have trimmed the "words of Jesus." We ask them to believe; then we try to persuade them to obey what they have professed. Writing on this text, Barclay said, "To learn to obey is the most important thing in life" (*The Gospel of Matthew*, vol. 1 [Philadelphia: Westminster Press, 1958], 297). The sense of the text is that "hearing the words" is not enough; to belong to Jesus, we have to "hear these words…and act on them."

III. The Words of Jesus Can Sustain Life in Testing Times.

The wise man built his house upon rock; the foolish fellow built his house on sand. I suspect the houses looked about the same when completed. The difference was hidden deep down and to all outward appearances, it made no difference.

However, "Every house is tested.… No man escapes temptation, testing, sorrow, or the claims of responsibility" (Buttrick, *The Interpreter's Bible*, vol. 7, 335). The storms of life are a poetic way of talking about losing a job, about a wife just walking away, about living with a husband who becomes a bum, about the sickness of a child, about the dreaded word after a physical examination. These testing times come.

There is a myth that circulates in our churches. If I do right, a good God will spare me hard testing, but in the nature of life, there are stormy times. The parable is about two builders and what happened to their houses. The one built on "rock," which means the truth that is in Jesus. The other built on "sand," which means ideas and values other than those found in Jesus. When the storms came, the truth that was in Jesus weathered the storm; the house stood. The other house fell. The flaw was in the foundation.

What do "these words of mine" mean? I think they mean the sum of all Jesus was, did, and said.

(1) Jesus is our very best picture of God.

(2) Jesus is the model of service. He was obedient to God. He did what God sent him to do. When we serve like Jesus, we serve both God and humankind.

(3) Jesus built an ethic on love. His new and great commandment was that we love one another. This world has too much stuff, but we don't have enough love.

(4) Jesus gave us a task. Go and tell. Build up the church. Do mercy and justice. Hurry the kingdom of God.

People of faith can give moving testimony. Many have told of the loss of a mate or the loss of a child. One family had their house blown away by a tornado. They literally describe the storms of life. All say essentially the same thing: In Christ they found the strength to pull themselves back together and go on. The foundation held.

IV. The Words of Jesus Are Better Than Other Foundations.

"And everyone who hears these words of mine and does not act on them will be like a foolish man who built his house on sand. The rain fell, and the floods came, and the winds blew and beat against that house, and it fell—and great was its fall!" (7:26-27). This part of the text is "politically incorrect." In a straightforward way Jesus said, "If you build your life on my words, your life can stand the storms. If you build on any other foundation, you are asking for trouble. My way is better."

There are places where Jesus is so beautiful…by our notions of beauty. When he tells us to feed the hungry, clothe the naked, and so on, Jesus is "in step" with many of the beliefs of our culture. Then Jesus suggests there are "sheep and goats," a heaven and a hell. He suggests his words are a better foundation for life than the words of anyone else. But if you think about what I'm doing, I'm measuring Jesus by the standards of our culture (he is beautiful; he's arrogant). As I understand the Bible, our culture is not going to measure Jesus. It is the other way around. The people who have advanced the Christian movement forward deeply believed that Jesus was "the way, and the truth, and the life. No one comes to the Father except through me" (Jn 14:6). Paul said it best: "According to the grace of God given to me, like a skilled master builder I laid a foundation, and someone else is building on it. Each builder must choose with care how to build on it. For no one can lay any foundation other than the one that has been laid; that foundation is Jesus Christ" (1 Cor 3:10-11).

HEALER

Matthew 9:27-38

ORIGINALLY PUBLISHED MARCH 17, 2002

Introduction

"Who Is This Jesus?" is our theme. In this lesson we identify Jesus as "Healer." Matthew meant for us to see Jesus as "Healer." Our text comes from a cluster of healing incidents Matthew has pulled together. To feel the power of the text and to catch the sense of what Matthew is trying to do, we need to see this text in the setting Matthew gave it.

- 8:1-4 Jesus healed a leper.
- 8:5-13 He healed the centurion's servant.
- 8:14-17 He healed Peter's mother-in-law.
- 8:28–9:1 He healed the Gadarene demoniacs.
- 9:2-8 A paralytic was healed.
- 9:18-26 He raised from the dead a little girl.
- 9:27-31 He made two blind men see.
- 9:32-34 He put a demon out of a mute man and made the man speak.

We would be missing something if we didn't ask ourselves, "What is Matthew trying to tell us in this series of healing stories?" I believe Matthew is answering our theme question. Healing is essential to identifying Jesus. Sometimes in our hurry to get to the teachings of Jesus, we almost skip over the healing stories. They create special problems; they strain our credulity. They raise all sorts of questions for a science-oriented public. But these stories of healing present questions we need to face. Once, theologians tied science in knots. The church restricted the study of the physical world, but now the tables are turned. Science is in the driver's seat. If the Bible speaks of miracles, then the Bible must be a primitive book that does not honor the scientific method. The scientific method of "knowing" is valuable, but it does not and cannot answer all questions. Where did I come from? What is right and wrong? Is there a God? What is going to happen to me when I die? Science does not handle these questions very well. Further, there are times when healing does not fit very well inside either the theological or the scientific box. People get well when doctors don't think they have a chance. People die when it looks like they are going to get well. Why? All around healing there is art, science, mystery, and God. The same God who made the rules doctors live by is the God who occasionally lays aside our rules and does what we label as a miracle. God made the rules; God can lay the rules aside and work beyond our understandings when God chooses. God gets to be God.

In this comment I will not dwell at length on a particular miracle. I'm no better at dissecting a miracle than you are, but I can pull at the themes in these healing stories that have a bearing on who Jesus is and how I'm supposed to act as a follower of Jesus.

I. Healing and Compassion.

Two ideas need to be emphasized. These ideas recur throughout Matthew 8 and 9.

Jesus was tireless in his compassion, but have you ever worked in a "night shelter"? When morning comes you are spent. Taking care of careless or helpless people burns energy like nothing else I know. Watch the way Matthew presents Jesus:

- "When Jesus had come down from the mountain, great crowds followed him; and there was a leper" (Mt 8:1).
- "When he entered Capernaum, a centurion came to him, appealing to him, and saying, 'Lord, my servant is…paralyzed' " (8:5).
- "When he entered Peter's house, he saw his mother-in-law lying in bed with a fever" (8:14).
- "When he came to the other side, to the country of Gadarenes, two demoniacs coming out of the tombs met him" (8:28).
- "And just then some people were carrying a paralyzed man lying on a bed. When Jesus saw their faith, he said to the paralytic" (9:1-2).

- "While he was saying these things to them, suddenly a leader of the synagogue came in…saying, 'My daughter has just died' " (9:18).
- "As Jesus went on from there, two blind men followed him, crying loudly, 'Have mercy on us, Son of David!' " (9:27-28).

These examples make my point. Sick people were constantly asking Jesus for help. He did not brush them off; amazingly, he kept responding. His compassion was nearly endless. I've worked in church offices where we acted like Jesus, and I've worked in places where you would never guess we had anything to do with Jesus. Compassion fatigue is common. The Apostle Paul said, "Brothers and sisters, do not be weary in doing what is right" (2 Thess 3:13). My inclination, when working with the poor, was to try to separate the worthy poor from the unworthy poor. This made me a detective, not a pastor. I did better when I just tried to respond like Jesus. Note the marginal people in the list of sick people. Lepers were at the edge of Jewish society. Centurions were associated with the hated Romans; that was not politically correct. Demon-possessed people were chained in the cemeteries. One man was "a leader of the synagogue" (9:18). He was in the mainstream of Jewish life, but the man was desperate. Under normal circumstances he probably would not have been open to Jesus.

Our churches have developed a painful pattern. We can be defined as pretty normal, middle-class Americans. We need to recognize that the healing compassion of Jesus extended to the down-and-out, the excluded foreigners, the frightening insane. I'm pretty good at working with people who are like me. The people at the edges are more difficult, and I've observed they are difficult for the church too. We need to work on that. Jesus was at home with people at the margins.

II. Healing and Power.

Matthew's message is clear. Miracles and the power it takes to accomplish a miracle identify Jesus as "Son of God." Eugene Boring said, "The miracle stories in 8:1–9:34 should not be interpreted in isolation, but each should be interpreted in the context of the section as a whole, since it has been constructed by Matthew as a single integrated unit presenting Jesus as 'Messiah in deed' (cf. 11:2), corresponding to 5:1–7:29 as 'Messiah in word' " (*The New Interpreter's Bible*, vol. 8 [Nashville: Abingdon Press, 1995], 222). Numerous commentators note that there are ten miracles cited in chapters 8–9, the same number of miracles Moses worked to free the Hebrews from

Egypt. As Moses freed God's people long ago, so Jesus frees people from their diseases in Matthew's time.

In our time we have put our own "spin" on the miracles of Jesus. We see a compassionate Christ who cared about hurting people. But Matthew lived in another time. His Gospel set out to tell people who Jesus was, and he carefully constructed his material to deliver his message. Matthew was very interested in our theme: "Who Is This Jesus?" Pulling together the miracles, presenting them in the way he did, was all for a purpose. Matthew is saying that because Jesus can heal, cast out demons, and raise a little girl from the dead, Jesus must be the Messiah and "Son of God."

The first 400 years of Christianity were defining. When Matthew wrote (around AD 75 to 80), people did not have a clear fix on who Jesus was. The church had not hammered out her theology. What is "old hat" for us was up for debate. Matthew's stories of healing were basic building blocks for the church as she built the theology we take for granted today.

One other idea needs to be included in this section on "Healing and Power." Several of the miracles have a comment about faith. "When Jesus saw their faith, he said to the paralytic" (9:2). When Jesus healed the centurion's servant, there is this faith comment: "Truly I tell you, in no one in Israel have I found such faith" (8:10b). And the woman who had the hemorrhage drew a word about faith: "Take heart, daughter; your faith has made you well" (9:22).

To what extent does our faith trigger Christ's healing or God's attention? I don't know the answer to my question, but the suggestion of this text is that our faith plays an important part in all God does for us. George Buttrick defined faith as "a native expectancy quickened in the course of man's experience by the promptings of God" (*The Interpreter's Bible*, vol. 7 [New York: Abingdon Press, 1951], 341). Faith assumes we are not alone, and the God who "is there" wants good for us. God is working in our lives for good. And when people of faith greeted Jesus, they saw in him help, hope, and the nearness of God. There was the possibility that their desperate situations could be relieved and their diseases healed. Faith is not magic that will wipe away pain, but faith in God may loose the goodness and power of God in ways beyond my imagining. God rarely works miracles on a fencepost. Then and now, God in Christ asks something of us even as we are asking of him.

III. Healing and Organization.

The conclusion of the "miracle chapters" is surprising. In verses 36-38 the text takes an unexpected turn. Two ideas you will want to consider:

(1) Jesus designed a strategy for caring and healing. All that had happened through chapters 8–9 is now compressed into a sentence. "When he saw the crowds he had compassion for them, because they were harassed and helpless" (9:36). Even Jesus, powerful and tireless as he was, could not reach or help all the "harassed and helpless." There had to be some way to multiply himself.

From chapter 10, "Then Jesus summoned the twelve…and gave them authority over unclean spirits, to cast them out, and to cure every disease and every sickness" (10:1). The rest of Matthew 10 is instruction to the Twelve about how they are to extend the ministry of Jesus. When disciples like you and me are at our best, we are extensions of the healing ministry of Jesus.

(2) Jesus elevated the laity. "The harvest is plentiful, but the laborers are few; therefore ask the Lord of the harvest to send out laborers into his harvest" (9:37-38). God's work is not going to be accomplished by just priests or preachers. There aren't enough of us, and too many people can't identify with us. Fishermen and tax collectors will have to enlist, be trained, and commissioned to task. Jesus fast-tracked twelve laymen into ministry. And what Jesus did is still happening. From churches today, laypeople are becoming missionaries for two weeks, God's carpenters for ten days, God's healers for a month. The job is getting done. The style is different, but the result is the same. People are being healed.

For Jesus, healing covered a lot of bases. It's not a narrow term that refers only to physical diseases. I can be sick in mind and spirit. When Jesus healed someone, he would often add a word that suggests what I am trying to say. He healed people in body and spirit. We need to do the same. Jesus healed all our broken parts.

The healing power of Jesus was extended to the apostles. In these days we leave healing to doctors. I have never sensed the power to heal in my work in ministry, but I'm more open to the idea today than I was thirty years ago. I pray for the sick with greater faith and hope. I think it is what I am supposed to do. This series is about defining Jesus, but as we define him, we also are marking the course we are supposed to follow. Think about it.

Following Jesus to Eat with Sinners

Matthew 9:9-13

ORIGINALLY PUBLISHED FEBRUARY 2, 1997

Introduction

Jesus surprised people all the time. Sometimes he bothered, offended. And the jolt in all this is that the more religious one was, the more Jesus surprised and jolted.

For nearly two thousand years people like me have been reading about and studying Jesus. We know he "ate with publicans and sinners," but most of us are more like Pharisees than we are like Jesus. We tend to run with church folks and avoid the places where today's "publicans and sinners" gather. This study is going to give us another lesson in the kind of person Jesus was and the way he went about "ministry." The hard part will be getting a congregation to loosen up and act out the kind of ministry Jesus practiced.

I see four ideas in our text that need lifting and explaining. Only the last one is absolutely essential. Use the others as they apply to your class. Always you remain the interpreter; at my best, I am your helper. Now let's open the Bible…

I. About Tax Collectors in the Roman World, 9:9a.

In every society, ours included, there is some onus, stigma attached to being a tax collector. But to be a Roman tax collector in Palestine in the first century was to shorten your list of friends. There wouldn't be many. And there were reasons:

(1) *The system invited corruption.* Each person who signed on to collect taxes was given a number. The Romans said, "We want you to gather this amount of money from this district." Anything gathered above that number went into the pocket of the tax collector. Nobody knew how much tax they were "supposed" to pay. They only knew what the tax collector was hitting them up to pay. And since nearly all tax collectors turned out to be rich, rich, rich…. You can see why people hated them so.

(2) *The people were taxed to poverty.* William Barclay lists the taxes everybody was supposed to pay in his explanation of this text. The list is too long, burdensome, oppressive (see William Barclay, *The Gospel of Matthew*, vol. 1 [Westminster Press, Philadelphia: 1958], 336-7). And when one was caught in a tax-heavy system, another tax collector was unliked and unwelcome. Especially was this so when the tax collector was gouging.

(3) *The Jews saw God as king.* They were strong nationalists. The presence of Rome and especially the taxation of Rome was to the Jews a special offense. They resented Rome. They hated Rome. And when they had a chance, they rebelled against Rome. For some Jews beating the Roman tax agent was akin to a religious service. It was not a sin; it was a virtue. But it was also a risk.

II. About Matthew, 9:9b.

The text is silent about any earlier contact between Matthew and Jesus. So, we could think this was the first time the two had seen each other. I think that unlikely. But since the text is silent, you know I am giving you my opinion here. This is not from the Bible.

(1) *Jesus was all around Galilee.* This "calling" took place at Capernaum. Jesus preached often there. Jesus did numerous miracles there. He was known. Almost certainly Matthew had had several chances to hear and watch Jesus.

(2) *Jesus attracted Matthew.* He was not just a money-grubbing, green-eyed, greedy man. Somewhere inside the man was the capacity to think unselfish, noble thoughts. Jesus saw this goodness inside Matthew.

(3) *Jesus appealed to best side of Matthew.* Jesus "said to him, 'Follow me.' And he got up and followed him" (Mt 9:9b). Every American can identify with the choice Matthew faced. He left financial security and he left the things money can buy. That was the price of following Jesus. I doubt the fishermen Jesus called left much in the way of comfort and security. But

Matthew did. One of the best lines in this lesson is the response of Matthew: "He got up and followed him." He didn't hesitate to think about it. He knew his mind. He chose Jesus.

III. Jesus Went to the Party, 9:10.

After Jesus called Matthew, there was a big party. Modestly Matthew does not tell us where the party took place, but Luke fills in what Matthew left out: "And he said to him, "Follow me." And he got up, left everything, and followed him. Then Levi [that is, Matthew] gave a great banquet for him in his house; and there was a large crowd of tax collectors and others sitting at the table with them" (Lk 5:29-29).

When Matthew decided to give it all up and follow Jesus, he threw a big party. And the party was not done to Pharisee specifications; everybody was invited. Matthew did not throw away his old friends when he went with Jesus.

The part we need to emphasize about "the party" is the way Jesus fit in. He was not there in judgment. He was there enjoying himself. He fit comfortably with everybody. I'm not sure I'm as much like Jesus as I ought to be. If I were at a country club where some are drinking but acting in a controlled, civil way, I could do fine. But you could get me in company where I would have a hard time.

In a way that is marvelous to me, Jesus put all kinds of people at ease. He did not kill the party. If he had, the Pharisees would not have raised a question. But Jesus was different in a wonderful way. He could be in the company of sinners, not sin and make sinners want to hear what he had to say. Tax collectors and sinners liked Jesus, wanted to hear more of him, enjoyed his company.

In contrast, Pharisees were suspicious of Jesus, fearful of what he might say or do, tried to entrap him and finally plotted to kill him. And they pulled it off. True to their nature, the Pharisees asked, "Why does your teacher eat with tax collectors and sinners?" (Mt 9:11). Because Jesus was socially comfortable with "tax collectors and sinners." If all Jesus did was socialize with "tax collectors and sinners," then we would conclude Jesus was a gregarious, party person. But as in all things about Jesus, there was purpose. He had a reason for what he was doing and he knew where he wanted a social contact to lead.

IV. Jesus Defines His Mission, 9:12-13.

This is the most important part of the lesson. The other points are of some value; this is the nut of the matter. Apparently the Pharisees were intimidated by Jesus. They asked "his disciples, 'Why does your teacher eat with tax collectors and sinners?' " (Mt 9:11). And the disciples carried the question to Jesus. Upon hearing the question, Jesus gave a direct, clear answer. What Jesus said ought to be written on every Sunday school class wall, on every pulpit, in a prominent place where deacons meet, a sign displayed where the officers of the mission groups gather, in the rooms where seminaries teach would-be preachers. The answer comes in three parts:

(1) *"Those who are well have no need of a physician, but those who are sick"* (Mt 9:12). This is an analogy. It is an illustration giving people a way to think. What if doctors said, "I can't go near sick people. It would be a reflection on my profession. After all, I am in the wellness business. To go near the sick would tarnish my reputation and make people wonder if I were sick myself." Foolishness. Of course doctors go near the sick. Doctors exist to tend and heal the sick.

Why did Jesus come? He came to "save us from sin." But by some convoluted, Pharisee way-of-thinking, Jesus is supposed to screen himself off from the very people he came to help. Strange. He came to help sinners, but he can't go near them.

(2) *"Go and learn what this means, 'I desire mercy, not sacrifice' "* (Mt 9:13a). There's a barb in this point. Jesus is saying, "Go back and check the Old Testament; if you know your Bible, you will understand what I mean." And what does he mean? Throughout the Old Testament the prophets kept telling the people…

> "I hate, I despise your festivals, and I take no delight in your solemn assemblies. Even though you offer me your burnt offerings and grain, I will not accept them.… But let justice roll down like waters, and righteousness like an ever-flowing stream. (Amos 5:21-24)

Micah said, "With what shall I come before the LORD… Shall I come before him with burnt offerings…? He has told you, O mortal, what is good; and what does the LORD require of you but to do justice, and to love kindness, and to walk humbly with your God" (Mic 6:6-8).

Isaiah said, "I have had enough of burnt offerings of rams and the fat of fed beasts; I do not delight in the blood of bulls, or of lambs.… Wash yourselves; make yourselves clean.… Cease to do evil, learn to do good; seek justice, rescue the oppressed, defend the orphan, plead for the widow" (Isa 1:10-17).

The short, sharp jab Jesus gave the Pharisees was this: You are supposed to know the Bible. But you missed the sense of it. "Go and learn what this means, 'I desire mercy, not sacrifice.' " Jesus was telling those people to go back to school and learn the first, strong meaning of all the prophets. Ritual religion is not as important to God as doing the right thing. And note that not all Pharisees are underground. They are in every church. Doing the ritual is more important than doing right.

(3) *"For I have come to call not righteous but sinners"* (Mt 9:13b). John Broadus, in his commentary on Matthew, said of this verse, "his conduct in associating with the very wicked accords with the design of his mission" (Commentary of *The Gospel of Matthew," An American Commentary on the New Testament,* vol. 1 [Philadelphia: The American Baptist Publication Society, 1886], 200-201). Jesus was "publicans and sinners" because it was for "publicans and sinners" he came. Before Jesus was born an angel told Joseph in a dream, "She will bear a son, and you are to name him Jesus, for he will save his people from their sins" (Mt 1:21). And it's hard to "save people from their sins" if you are unwilling to touch the people you came to save.

Always church people need to "get in touch" with this text. The Pharisee spirit is not dead; it travels incognito. Always we are tempted to close the church. We want pure people like us…and no more lest we be dirtied by associating with the unwashed. So churches become clubs rather than the open, inviting, serving places Jesus meant them to be. Let's try to use this lesson to open our churches to all people Jesus touched. And if we do, we will have a diverse company when we gather on a Sunday morning. This will not dilute our message; it will give us an audience for it.

Our Call: Sheep in the Midst of Wolves

Matthew 10:5-23

ORIGINALLY PUBLISHED AUGUST 27, 1995

Introduction

Today's lesson comes from Jesus' sending out of the twelve in Matthew 10. The instructions were clear and straightforward: "Go...[and] proclaim the good news, 'The kingdom of heaven has come near' " (Mt 10:5, 7). Jesus goes on to say to the twelve that they are sent out like "sheep into the midst of wolves." Sheep are vulnerable. They need protection and guidance from the dangers of the world, including the wolf. Well, that's you and me too. We are the sheep. Jesus sends us out and we do a good work for the Lord only if we follow his guidance and trust his protection.

This text has a lot to offer. Sometimes it is helps to take a few steps back look at it all in perspective, from a distance. If you take a few steps back you might see how this commissioning of the twelve in Matthew 10 has roots going back all the way to Matthew 5, the Sermon on the Mount. For this lesson, let's start with Matthew 10, explore it, get to know it, and pick the fruit. Then let's follow the roots back to Matthew 5, the Sermon on the Mount. Then we will be looking at the whole thing.

I. Where Should They Go? 10:5-6.

Jesus first tells the disciples to "Go nowhere among the Gentiles." This seems kind of a strange thing to hear from the one who later said "Go therefore and make disciples of all nations" (Mt 28:19) What could this mean? Did

Jesus change his mind or was the gospel not for the Gentile? Sherman E. Johnson in *The Interpreter's Bible* helps us out a bit. Some translations read this verse as "Go not into the way of the Gentiles, and into any city of the Samaritans enter ye not" (Mt 10:5 KJV). Johnson explains that the "way of the Gentile" is probably a road leading to a Gentile city. Jews were not allowed "to go on such a road at the time of a pagan festival if the road led only to the Gentile city" (Sherman E. Johnson, *The Interpreter's Bible.* vol. 7, Nashville: Abingdon Press, 1979: 364). Of course the gospel is for everyone, but Jesus knew some ground was sometimes more fertile than others.

Telling the disciples not to go on the "way of the Gentiles" was simply shrewd leadership. The cause of the gospel would not be advanced by breaking laws about what roads were to be traveled. Remember, Jesus sent them out as "Sheep in the Midst of Wolves" and they were to be "wise as serpents and innocent as doves" (Mt 10: 16). He was saying to them "Be smart! Don't do anything that's going to get in the way of your proclaiming the Kingdom of God." That's a message that needs to be heard today. Be smart! Be wise! God is trying to do something big and all he has is us to do it with. Don't do something that can hamper enlarging God's kingdom.

Scholars speculate as to why they were only to go to the "lost sheep of the house of Israel" (Mt 10:6). Sherman Johnson once again helps us out by suggesting that the phrase "lost sheep of the house of Israel" refers to the Amhaarez or "country people" (*The Interpreter's Bible.* vol. 7 [Nashville: Abingdon Press, 1979], 365). These would have been the folks who live outside of the Gentile cities. Country people have a way about them of being relaxed, "laid back" to use a modern phrase. Country people back then were a little more relaxed too. They were not as concerned with the details of the law and that made them none too popular with the Pharisees. So whatever the details were behind Jesus giving the twelve the instructions to go to the "lost sheep of the house of Israel," it just makes sense to do so since they would likely be predisposed to hear the message about the Kingdom coming near. That makes good sense for us today too. You can't reach the world all at once, so go where you have better chances of being effective. That would seem right for those who were "wise as serpents" (Mt 10:16).

II. What Should They Do? 10:7-15.

Jesus laid out the plan in straightforward terms.

- "proclaim the good news, 'The kingdom of heaven has come near' " (Mt 10:7) Not much has changed since that is what you and I are about: proclaiming the good news of Jesus.
- "cure the sick, raise the dead, cleanse the lepers, cast out demons" (Mt 10:8). Jesus gave the twelve the power to do what he had done. Jesus empowers us too. We would be surprised a great deal at what all we could do if only we were committed enough to following Jesus and God's call on our lives.
- "Take no gold, or silver, or copper…" (Mt 10:9ff). They were to go with what they had. We could learn from this. If we spend all of our time getting ready to do something big it will probably never happen.
- "As you enter the house, greet it…If anyone will not welcome you or listen to your words, shake off the dust from your feet as you leave…." (Mt 10:12-14). Jewish custom held that if a Jew was in an unclean place, they should dust their feet and not carry that uncleanness to a place that is clean. A larger message could be that not everybody is going to welcome a word from the Lord. When that happens, we should move on and keep being about our Lord's business.

III. How Can They Do It? 10:16-23.

These verses start out with the words that give our lesson its title. "See, I am sending you out like sheep into the midst of wolves…" (Mt 10:16). Taken together, all the verses in this section bring home a theme: it will not be easy but I am with you. Jesus is preparing them for the obstacles they will likely face. It's interesting what road blocks are ahead. Government leaders, religious leaders—even family—can be expected to try to hold up those who make efforts to spread the news of the Kingdom of heaven.

Jesus tells them that when that happens don't worry. It's as if he is saying "God will be with you and even help you say the right thing." Jesus says to them that it is God who is speaking through them. I wonder how our Sunday mornings would sound both in preaching and in Sunday school if we all remembered that God wants to speak through us.

IV. The Roots, 5:1-23.

The kind of discipleship to which Jesus called the twelve is an enlarged expression of what he taught at the Sermon on the Mount. Taken together we can have an even bigger picture of what it means to be called by God.

(1) *Gentle Spirit,* 5:1-12, Jesus began the Sermon on the Mount with the Beatitudes. The sense of the Beatitudes is that God is going to have a special care for, a favor toward the people who have a certain kind of attitude. Jesus did not just say, "You need a new attitude." Rather, he spelled out what kind of attitude that would be. Take a look at the Beatitudes when they are put a different way:

- "Blessed are the poor in spirit"…God is going to take care of you.
- "Blessed are those who mourn"…God is going to take care of you.
- "Blessed are the meek"…God is going to take care of you.
- "Blessed are those who hunger and thirst for righteousness"…God is going to take care of you.

And on until the end I could go. The sense is that God is looking for a new attitude, a new spirit.

There is not one word about theological correctness, about judgment, about including or excluding. All the virtues Jesus wants in the "new disciple" are bent toward a gentle spirit. Put this against the orthodoxy of the day when Jesus lived. He was followed around by people who were checking him, questioning him, almost interrogating him. The Pharisee spirit overpowered the kindness and the compassion that was in "the Law and the prophets." Jesus got back in touch with that compassion. His disciples were "called" to a new spirit. The Beatitudes define that spirit. This is the way I summarize the Beatitudes text and apply it to "the call" of the disciples.

(2) *A Public Obligation,* 5:13-16. What Jesus has asked us to do is attractive. Deep down inside we all are drawn to the ideals of the Beatitudes. They are right and good and true. But if we embrace them we are liable for ridicule to profess them and then not be able to live up to them. So, there is the option of a middle ground. We can follow Jesus, but we can do it privately. Private religion spares us ridicule from "the world" and the charge of hypocrisy if we fall short of our profession. We become "Nicodemus disciples." We come to Jesus, but we come by night (see John 3:2).

Jesus wants none of private discipleship. He told his disciples their profession was public; they were expected to "be witnesses" (see Acts 1:8). Another Matthew text put the idea even more strongly: "Everyone therefore who acknowledges me before others, I also will acknowledge before my Father in heaven, but whoever denies me before others, I also will deny before my Father in heaven" (Mt 10:32-33).

Too much religion is privatized. We are looking for our salvation, our family, our community, our church, etc. Here we are put to larger tasks. All that is happening in our world is our work. Justice and peace, truth and virtue: these are things we are to preserve by incarnation. We are to "in flesh" these endangered ideas/virtues. This we "are called" to do.

Underlying all the Bible is a constant theme: sin is going to ruin this world unless God and the people of God save her. Jesus came to save. All who follow Jesus are saving agents in our world. This is what we are "called" to do. Jesus was public; we are to be public. Jesus caught all kinds of grief for being public; we may catch a little of that grief, too. It is a part of discipleship…and always has been.

(3) *A New Understanding*, 5:17-23. This part of our text is "a call" to a new understanding of what was the sense of the law. First, we will see Jesus lay down some principles. Second, we will see Jesus illustrate a "new understanding" by reinterpreting one of the Ten Commandments.

- *Principles/convictions about the Scripture*, 5:17-20. "Do not think that I have come to abolish the law or the prophets; I have come…to fulfill" (Mt 5:17). Jesus had as high an opinion of the Old Testament as any of his accusers.
- *The law will endure.* "Until heaven and earth pass away, not one letter, not one stroke of a letter, will pass from the law until all is accomplished" (Mt 5:18).
- *To teach and to do the law ensures greatness in the kingdom of heaven.* "Whoever does them and teaches them will be called great in the kingdom of heaven" (Mt 5.19). To this point his listeners would have been in complete agreement. No surprises. But just before he left a series of affirmations about believing in "the law," Jesus said what would have truly amazed his audience. "For I tell you, unless your righteousness exceeds that of the scribes and Pharisees, you will never enter the kingdom of heaven" (Mt 5:20). It was a bombshell! It was radical. The people who put themselves forward as being the most zealous keepers of "the law" were now falling short of minimum righteousness. They were not going to make it to heaven. They were missing the mark. They were trying very hard to please God but not doing it.

Then Jesus begins a radical reinterpretation of "the law." This reinterpretation will run through the end of Matthew 5. Our text uses but one illustration of this radical reinterpretation. "You have heard that it was said to those of ancient times, 'You shall not murder' and 'whoever murders shall be liable to judgment.' *But I say to you* that if you are angry with a brother or a sister, you will be liable to judgment..." (Mt 5:21-22).

Jesus is reinterpreting the law. Does he believe the law? Very much. But he is giving the law new meaning. He is breaking with tradition (as the Pharisees defined tradition). Most of our churches are not yet ready to take Jesus seriously at the point of some of his radical understandings of what the law was really meant to be. Jesus was not breaking law; by his own word he was "fulfilling" law (see 5:17b).

Jesus took the old law and filled it with new meaning. We are still working toward the Jesus understandings.

Conclusion

The disciples were "called" to special service quite as much as Abraham, Mary, and Ezekiel. In the sending of the Twelve and the Sermon on the Mount, Jesus lines out the hard road and the high road they are to follow:

(1) "The call" to go.

(2) "The call" to be wise and not waste time.

(3) "The call" to do nothing that will stand in the way of the gospel.

(4) "The call" to discipleship is a call to a gentle spirit.

(5) "The call" to discipleship is a call to a public obligation.

(6) "The call" to discipleship is a call to a new understanding of what the law and the prophets were all about.

While we had to stretch to apply Abraham, Mary, and Ezekiel's call to our own, we have no trouble at all giving immediate application of this text. What Jesus asked of them is what he is asking of us.

Following Jesus Outside the Law

Matthew 12:1-8

ORIGINALLY PUBLISHED FEBRUARY 9, 1997

Introduction

You remember how Jesus put aside the social customs of the religious establishment and ate with "publicans and sinners." Pharisees did not approve. But at heart, I suspect thoughtful Pharisees respected Jesus for reaching out, getting in touch with the part of the Jewish community that was cut off from temple and synagogue life. Nicodemus, a member of the religious establishment, must have been an admirer, perhaps a secret follower, of Jesus. People like Nicodemus knew Jesus was in touch with all that was good and right and true in the Old Testament when he ministered to people cut off from God.

Today's lesson is another matter. Here Jesus is challenging more than social custom. He is defending his disciples when they have clearly broken Old Testament law. So in this lesson we will "Follow Jesus Outside the Law," but we will do more. Is the Old Testament authority for a New Testament Christian? If so, how? How could Jesus say, "Do not think that I have come to abolish the law or the prophets; I have come not to abolish but to fulfill" (Mt 5:17). So, to "Follow Jesus Outside the Law," is to raise a question about the way Jesus treated and respected the Old Testament. That is also a part of this lesson.

This lesson has practical application. We live in a time when Sunday is treated like Monday (or Saturday). American social custom has just about killed any sacred day. What does this mean to a serious Christian? A casual member of a church I served said to me, "I come to church when I don't have anything else to do." And his pattern supported his statement. Jesus was trying to uproot the legalism of the Pharisees. But we don't live in a legalistic society. We live in a permissive society. I wonder how Jesus would teach this lesson. He was contending with Pharisees who had a rule-ridden religion. We are dealing with people who are anything but Pharisees...they are more likely to be permissive than legalistic.

I. The Law on Sabbath Observance.

The law of Moses reads like this: "Remember the sabbath day, and keep it holy. Six days you shall labor and do all your work. But the seventh day is a sabbath to the LORD your God; you shall not do any work" (Ex 20:8-10a). Saturday was the Sabbath. No one was supposed to work on Saturday. It was a day set apart for rest. Hopefully, it would also be a day for worship and reflection.

But what was "work"? The Jews were deep into definition. So what constituted work had to be lined out for everyone; nothing could be left loose or hanging. William Barclay gives us the detail we need to teach this lesson:

> Thirty-nine basic actions were laid down, which were forbidden on the Sabbath, and amongst them were reaping, winnowing and threshing, and preparing a meal....
>
> By their conduct the disciples were guilty of far more than one breach of the Law. By plucking the corn they were guilty of reaping; by rubbing it in their hands they were guilty of threshing; by separating the grain and the chaff they were guilty of winnowing; and by the whole process they were guilty of preparing a meal on the Sabbath day, for everything which was to be eaten on the Sabbath had to be prepared the day before. (Barclay, *The Gospel of Matthew,* vol. 2 [Westminster Press, Philadelphia: 1958], 24-25)

Now to the text: "At that time Jesus went through the grainfields on the sabbath; his disciples were hungry, and they began to pluck heads of grain and to eat" (Mt 12:1). Here's what happened:

(1) Rows were created in grain fields for passage. Jesus and the disciples were walking on a path through the field.

(2) It was a sabbath day, and the disciples were hungry. They reached out, plucked the "heads of grain," rubbed the grain between their hands and ate.

(3) Pharisees were following along the path. They saw what the disciples had done. It was a clear violation of defined Old Testament law. Gotcha!

So the statement that amounted to an accusation: "Look, your disciples are doing what is not lawful to do on the sabbath" (Mt 12:2). And in any Jewish court of law, the disciples were guilty as charged. They were breaking the law of Moses. More important, they were breaking the Law of God. This lesson is not a study in redefining the law of Moses to make it appear the disciples did not break the law. They did break the law. What will Jesus say/do now?

II. How Jesus Justified Breaking Sabbath Law.

Seems to me Jesus used four arguments to clear his disciples of wrongdoing. They are…

(1) *History.* In 1 Samuel 21:1-6 David was in flight from King Saul. He had a small band of faithful who were with him. They were hungry. David went into the tabernacle at Nob and asked the priest Ahimelech for bread. There was no bread except five loaves, "only holy bread" (1 Sam 21:4). But because of David's extreme need, the holy bread was given David. And no blame was attached to David's actions. Jesus cited this example to the Pharisees from the history of the Jewish people.

(2) *Pattern.* "Have you not read in the law that on the sabbath the priests in the temple break the sabbath and yet are guiltless?" (Mt 12:5). Every Sabbath temple priests killed and prepared animals for sacrifice, lifted the dead animals onto the altar and did all manner of other chores. It was the duty of the Temple, and it happened every day. No one accused Temple priests of breaking the law, but they did so every Saturday. It was a pattern.

(3) *Principle.* "If you had known what this means, 'I desire mercy and not sacrifice,' you would not have condemned the guiltless" (Mt 12:7). The key phrase is "mercy not sacrifice." Throughout the prophets there was the constant drumbeat: Your rituals are not getting through to God. God wants mercy and justice and truth and service…more than God wants liturgy and ritual and form and sacrifice.

(4) *Priority.* The last argument in defense of the disciples is more subtle and I think more powerful. Jesus said, "I tell you something greater than the temple is here" (Mt 12:6). We see this statement through the eyes of two thousand years of interpretation by the Christian community. So, our vision is colored, preconditioned. But Jesus was quietly identifying himself. He was greater than the Temple, and events have proven it. He was more worthy of worship than anything in the Temple. He was a clearer revelation of God than the religion practiced at the Temple. Priority. Jesus is our High Priest (see Heb 8:1).

The arguments Jesus used did not convince his accusers. They were locked into a way of thinking that made them deaf to a new word from God. But what Jesus said informs the Church and lays the groundwork for the application of this teaching.

III. What Are We to Do with the Christian Sabbath?

Some people are going to take this teaching and run with it. When they get through running, there will be no sacred day. I am not among that crowd. But I don't want to be a legalist either. Let me try to find a place to stand that is between the two poles of legalism and "anything goes."

(1) *Notice what the disciples did with the Jewish Sabbath.* After Jesus went back to heaven and after the Church was up and going, the disciples began to worship on Sunday instead of Saturday. Resurrection Day seemed more important to them than the strict law of Moses. So, the disciples did away with all Jewish sabbath rule AND they quit the seventh day as their sacred, holy day. (I am aware of that part of the Christian community who do not agree with what the disciples did. So we have Seventh-Day Adventists, Seventh-Day Baptists, etc.)

(2) *We are not slaves of the Sabbath; we are to use it for good…whatever this involves.* Now Paul becomes our teacher. All rule that is pressed down on the Church in a legalistic way is in violation of the Spirit of Christ. He has set us free. All of Galatians is about this new freedom in Christ. So, when I go to a soup kitchen and help the hungry and lift and sweat, set tables and wash dishes, I am doing the work of Christ. And if this be done on a Sunday (or a Saturday), no matter.

A personal illustration. The year was 1980. On a Thursday Dr. Jess Chapman discovered in Dot a threatening lump. On Friday further examination confirmed what Dr. Chapman had suspected. On a Sunday afternoon Dr. Chapman, with a support team, performed surgery on Dot. Happily, she has been clear from then until now. The work was done on a Sunday. No one criticized me, Dot, or Dr. Chapman. All understood need overrode religious rule.

(3) *We need a day apart, a sacred day.* The trouble with this lesson is that the wrong people are likely to hear it. If one is looking for a way to get out of church and get free of religious obligation, this text could be your out. If that is one's inclination, I think such person is misreading the text.

Before World War I trains did not run on Sunday, no stores were open on Sunday, games were not played on Sunday nor movies open. One by one "Blue Laws" have come down; Sunday is a religious day for only a minority.

I wonder how Jesus would approach our situation. How would he teach this lesson to Americans these days? I don't know the answer to my question. But let me give you my opinion...

- Christian people need pattern. We need to have a time set apart for worship of God and fellowship with the community of faith. Break the pattern long enough, and you will damage faith. Look at the pattern of so many who move away and quit going to church. And slowly a pagan pattern becomes the way of life for these people.
- Worship/fellowship is essential to Christian health. Going to church is not just something the preacher presses down on you. It is good for your soul. I need to forgive the people who have offended me; I need to be forgiven my sins. This happens when I worship. I need to be lifted to noble thoughts. I need to get in touch with my highest promises...and pledge again to keep them. I need to put myself in a place where God can whisper new instructions to me, lead me to new paths of service.
- The church needs the presence and care of her people.
- We can't "do church" by sending a check once a month. We have to show our faces. We have to give the institution some TLC. We have to weed gardens and tend the institutions that hold high our strongest values.
- Our children need a model from us on Sunday. When the rest of the kids are "out to play," our kids wonder why they can't go out to play Sunday morning too. What do you tell them? The answer is not a word or teaching. Our answer is a pattern. Quietly but with strength, mother and daddy set a steady example for the children. Every Sunday it is off to church. This speaks loudly to children of what matters to parents. Then in the next generation grandparents can watch another generation "go to church."

Conclusion

I suspect some of you think I am just an old Pharisee. Not really. I am a dead-serious churchman intent on helping people to be free of legalism and deeply rooted in Christ and his Church. I want both.... And I think Jesus wanted both, too.

Following Jesus on the Water

Matthew 14:22-33

ORIGINALLY PUBLISHED FEBRUARY 16, 1997

Introduction

Today's lesson is a window into the private instruction of the disciples. It is an experience that cannot be duplicated. So, none of us is literally going to "Follow Jesus on the Water." But that does not mean this text has nothing for us. Actually, I think there are some parts of this lesson that will translate into life more immediately than others. So, as you open this study, consider…

- Surely a good part of life is into the wind. This text tells of the disciples struggling with a situation where "the wind was against them."
- Often I over-step my faith or my capacity. I want to do what Jesus did. I fail. What then? Am I a loss, a no-good? Is there a place in Christian service for people who "can't walk on water"?
- Where is Jesus when life gets hard? Is he accessible, available, near, caring? And the lesson has an answer for us.

I think you see the same possibilities in this text I do. Now let's open and apply some of the teachings. Remember the rules. You are the interpreter. I am your helper. Sometimes I will make mistakes. Catch them and correct them and keep them from your class. But when I help you, build that part into the lesson. The best help for Bible interpreters is the Spirit of God. The same Spirit who inspired the writers will draw near to you when you interpret and apply. Listen. Follow your own insights. Sometimes they come from the Spirit. And use your own good sense.

I. Time Alone, 14:22-23.

Context is important in the opening verses of this lesson. Jesus has just "fed the five thousand." Read 14:13-21 for the full picture. Obviously the crowd is impressed with both food and miracle. They want more. It is in this setting that our lesson begins. But Jesus does not do the "popular" thing. He did not try to build on the acclaim and crowd-pleasing effect of the miracle. Rather, he did an unpolitical thing. In two distinct acts Jesus separated himself from being a popular or political Messiah.

(1) *"Immediately he made the disciples get into the boat and go on ahead to the other side…"* (Mt 14:22a). The "other side" means the other side of Lake Galilee. But that is not the part I want you to see. "He made the disciples…go on ahead." I think the disciples would have preferred Jesus to linger and soak up the praise and acclaim. They would have enjoyed it had Jesus decided to "make political hay" of the feeding of the multitude. The more popularity Jesus gathered, the better the disciples like it. Jesus made them go away. Remember the temptations of Jesus. One of the Devil's ploys with Jesus was to offer him rule over this world (see Mt 4:8-10). That temptation would appear in several forms in the ministry of Jesus. The disciples were sometimes unwitting agents of the Devil to urge that temptation on Jesus.

(2) *"He dismissed the crowds"* (Mt 14:22b). Crowds were fickle. Sometimes they flocked to Jesus. Other times they drifted away from him. Jesus was not a late-twentieth-century performer. Such people feed off the crowd. They live to be before a crowd. They cannot live apart from the adulation of a crowd. So, whatever it takes to keep the crowd, that is what such people are willing to do. Some preachers are more modern entertainers than they know. They have to get and hold the crowd. It is what "winds their clock."

Jesus was a different sort. He seems to have distrusted the crowd. Perhaps he distrusted himself with the crowd. He was intent on being driven by inner voices than by outer praise. The crowd had to go. Jesus had to get in touch with the One who really motivated him.

He sent the disciples on ahead to "the other side" of the lake. He would meet them later. He dismissed the crowd. And then the text gets to the place Jesus was going all the time. "When evening came, he was there alone…" (Mt 14:23b). Jesus was sent from God. He was commissioned to do the work of God. He lived to serve God. He was willing to be spent for God. And regularly he had to have time alone. Most often this time is filled with prayer. Sometimes I suspect he just sat still, thought, pondered, meditated.

I have not put a phone in my car. You may think me primitive or strange. But when I am alone in the car, I can think. Not all my thoughts are religious. But most of them are purposeful. Dot and I rarely turn on the TV until evening. Constant radio and TV and phone keep me from reflection. Occasionally they keep me from prayer. Jesus was pulled by disciples and crowd to be less than God wanted him to be. He had to get off by himself and think about it. He had to take a compass reading. He had to check to see if he was on course. He made some time alone. This is more than an observation. This is a pattern I need to follow. I hope you can urge this idea on your class. There is spiritual health in the practice. Especially when tempted to "please the crowd," get away from those people. Get by yourself. Get very still. Get as near to God as you can.

II. Take Courage, 14:24-27.

Lake Galilee is notorious for sudden, violent storms. On the night Jesus sent the disciples "to the other side" of the lake, one of these storms "came up." The text reads, "but by this time the boat, battered by the waves, was far from the land, for the wind was against them" (Mt 14:24). Matthew has condensed events.

Apparently in the early evening the disciples set out by boat for "the other side" of the lake. But they were caught. Maybe it was a storm. Maybe they were just unlucky enough to be rowing into a strong wind. Either way, it was a slow go. John's Gospel helps us fill in the blanks. Lake Galilee is about four-and-a-half miles across. John, writing of the same event, says, "When they had rowed about three or four miles…" (Jn 6:19). Rowing is hard work when the wind is against you. They had been at it for a long time. By now it was three or four o'clock in the morning. Fatigue, frustration and perhaps a little fear are in the disciple band. It was not a good time.

Get the setting. Yesterday afternoon they were on "cloud nine." They were serving at the "feeding of the five thousand." Now they are rowing as hard as they can. They may be in real danger. As far as they were concerned, they should have stayed with the crowd and turned crowd approval into political opportunity (see John 6:15 to confirm the crowd's intention).

This part of the story is the part most like life. All of us have had times when "the wind was against us." Some of the people in the class are in such times right now. A religion that is no good when "the wind is against me," is not a religion that will help. And so disoriented were the disciples in their fatigue, frustration and fear until even when Jesus came near they did not recognize him. "They were terrified, saying, 'It is a ghost!' " (Mt 14:26). We don't think straight when we are worn and worried. There's all kinds of application for this truth. I tell women who have become widows, "Don't make any serious, big decisions for six months. Wait until grief lets up a little. You will think clearer and make better decisions. The disciples make the point. They were not in a position to recognize even the Lord they had risked all to follow. Fear can do that to us all.

Then out of nowhere, "early in the morning he came walking toward them on the sea" (Mt 14:25a). Jesus was there. And one of the powerful teachings in this lesson is the Jesus who shows up at the right time every time. And this is not accident. It is the way Jesus is. So…

- Are you a small, struggling company of Christians trying to "make it"? "Where two or three are gathered in my name, I am there among them" (Mt 18:20). Jesus is there.
- Are you seriously trying to live out the Great Commission? Then remember the closing lines: "And remember, I am with you always, to the end of the age" (Mt 28:20b).
- Are you frightened by life and afraid of the things you "are supposed to do"? This is the Jesus who promised to send us a Comforter…the Spirit of God who will make all the parts of the journey with us.

And when "the wind is against us" and he comes near, what does he say? "Take heart, it is I; do not be afraid" (Mt 14:27). This text is for me. I need it. I lean on it and draw strength from it. Three short ideas and everyone of them is packed with power…

(1) *Take heart.* The literal meaning of the Greek is "take courage." The world is filled with frightened people. Anyone with courage can lead, inspire, change. Jesus gives us heart, courage.

(2) *It is I.* When the disciples knew who was walking on the water, everything began to make sense. So often Jesus is near, nearer than we know, and we miss the signal…and are afraid.

(3) *Do not be afraid.* All through the Bible we are counseled not to fear. John said love would take away fear. Paul told Timothy not to give in to his fears. Jesus tells the disciples to get past fear. Fear paralyzes governments, churches, people. And when we can take Jesus to heart and "not be afraid," we can be about his business. Until we get past our fears, we are pretty close to useless.

III. Testing Peter, 14:28-32.

The last paragraph in our text narrows. It is all about Peter. As always, Peter is both daring and foolish, filled with courage and overcome by fear. And this text only confirms what we already know about him.

It was dark. The disciples were not sure the one they saw "walking toward them on the sea" was really Jesus. Also their vision was distorted by their frustration and fear. So, Peter asks confirmation: "Lord, if it is you, command me to come to you on the water" (Mt 14:28). And Jesus took him up on it. Straightway Jesus said, "Come" (Mt 14:29a).

It is small miracle when Jesus walks on the water. We expect such of him. Always the laws of nature were at his command; that's how he did miracles. But when Peter walks on water, that's different. Big miracle. And for a little, Peter really did "walk on the water, and came toward Jesus" (Mt 14:29b). But then he did the most normal, human thing, he noticed the strong wind…became frightened…began to sink" (Mt 14:30). Jesus reach out, steadied him and the two of them "got into the boat" (Mt 14:31-32a). What are we to make of this? What does it mean?

(1) *Jesus defined Peter's problem.* It was not a matter of gravity taking over and Peter sinking like any normal person should. No. Jesus said Peter's experiment in "walking on water" broke down because his faith broke down. "You of little faith, why did you doubt?" (Mt 14:31b).

More often than not, the faith experiments we do attempt for God break down for want of faith more than they break down from natural causes. More good things are not attempted by churches from fear than from inability. We can do far more than ever we dare to attempt for God. We spend way too much time "noticing the strong wind." The power of the Risen Christ is there all the time. We just need some people who have the nerve to "get out of the boat" and walk "toward Jesus."

(2) *But the entire episode had one positive effect.* Who Jesus was came clearer to the disciples than ever before. "And those in the boat worshipped him, saying, 'Truly you are the Son of God' " (Mt 14:33). Jesus did miracles for more than one reason. He helped Peter to the boat and two things came of it:

• Peter was saved from the sea.
• Jesus was identified for all the disciples.

In these days it is stylish to emphasize reason number 1. Helping people is the reason for the miracles of Jesus. That is there. But where we put the emphasis is highly cultural. Helping people is "in." Doing good is favored. Public opinion likes to take theology out of church and put good works in. That is the bent of our time. But always the Bible is taking the long look. Identifying Jesus and "worshipping him" is far more important than our secular society cares to note.

At root, the bottom line, fundamental to everything in the Christian religion, is figuring out who Jesus is. When we do identify him as Lord of all, as Savior and Master, as Messiah and King…then we are truly Christian. We worship him and follow him and are willing to serve him. Miracles have helped the dim-sighted to see Jesus for who he is. There is a sense in which all of us make the same journey the disciples did. We are drawn to Jesus. We are amazed by Jesus. Then out of some experience that defines him clearly, we come to worship him and make him the Lord of our lives. This text takes us where we all need to go.

Following Jesus Up the Mountain

Matthew 17:1-8

ORIGINALLY PUBLISHED FEBRUARY 23, 1997

Introduction

"The Transfiguration" of Jesus is our subject, and few passages in all the Gospels admit of so many interpretations. I will not sort out the variations and tell you which is right and which is wrong. That belongs in the province of wiser people. But I can pick out some of the several meanings in this text, and hold them up for your examination.

In the first instance, I believe "The Transfiguration" is a genuine, historical event. It happened as the Gospels say it did. The reason I even mention this is because some commentaries do not. Some hold this was a dream of the disciples or an invention of the church to enlarge the image of Jesus. I disagree. The life of Jesus is sprinkled with events that are beyond the realm of what we would call "normal." He was "the miracle worker." From his birth to his ascension God was laying aside the rules of the natural order.

I will list four strong ideas in this text. Each could be the full subject for your lesson. Each would provide enough material for a good sermon. But rather than down-sizing the text and majoring on one part (or teaching), I've chosen to give you the four big ideas I see (and there could be more I do not see).

Now for some contextual comment. It is late in the ministry of Jesus. The public ministry is done. Jesus has taken the disciples on a long, almost private retreat. At Caesarea Philippi he asked them, "Who do people say that the Son of Man is?" (Mt 16:13b). Peter correctly identifies Jesus. "You are the Messiah, the Son of the living God" (Mt 16:16). Then Jesus told the disciples the cross was before him, and he began to school them for the life they would lead after he was gone away from them. I suggest you read all of Matthew 16 before you teach.

And then "six days later, Jesus took with him Peter and James and his brother John and led them up a high mountain, by themselves" (Mt 17:1) Where was this? Probably "the Transfiguration" took place on the slopes of Mount Hermon. We will never know for sure. But the setting makes sense with the other geographical references.

Here are the four ideas that seem to me to catch the sense of this profound event/teaching. Always you are the interpreter; I am your helper. I hope you use what I write; that makes me useful. But never let me become a crutch.

I. Lifted, 17:2.

The text reads, "And he was transfigured before them, and his face shone like the sun, and his clothes became dazzling white" (Mt 17:2). So, the face of Jesus "glowed with the transcendent glory reserved for heavenly beings" (*The New Interpreter's Bible,* vol. 8 [Nashville: Abingdon Press, 1995], 363). This was not the first time the Bible tells about the face glowing, shining. When Moses came down from Mount Sinai, he did not know "that the skin of his face shone because he had been talking with God" (Ex 34:29). The clear suggestion is that Jesus (and three disciples who were with him) was lifted heavenward, moved for a brief season into another realm.

My first thought upon reading this text went something like this: How in the world can I make this text useful to ordinary people like us? I've never been "transfigured." Most of you would be slow to claim you had had any experience that would compare to our text. But then I began to think. Have I ever been lifted? Have the blinders of humanity ever been taken from my face for a time? Has my preoccupation with the mundane, the daily ever been eclipsed by a higher vision? And the truth is all of us have had such "lifted" moments.

Now let me define a "lifted" moment. Isaac Watts gave us great hymns. He wrote over six thousand of them. But when you look in our hymnbooks, you will see but fifteen, sixteen still in use. Watts lived three hundred years ago. Culture, world view, science, church: everything has changed in those three hundred years. But fifteen or so of his hymns can transcend all that has changed and still inspire today's worship. They still speak to us. I think Isaac

Watts was "lifted" when he wrote "When I Survey the Wondrous Cross," don't you? Whenever it was, whatever the setting, whoever was around him (or not around him), Watts was "lifted" out of himself in that moment. He was inspired, and we are better for it.

And what of George Frederick Handel and the creation of "The Messiah"? Surely it was a "lifted" moment for him, and all Christians are the better for it. And on and on this sort of illustration could run. I've preached hundreds of sermons. Most were pretty ordinary. But occasionally, once in awhile, I've been "lifted." I've preached better than I can preach. I was "lifted." I came near to the Presence of God. The Spirit came near and "lifted" my earth-trapped mind. I drew near the heavenly, and I had real insight.

We will not be invited to join a small, select band and walk up Mount Hermon. That was reserved for Peter, James and John. But the experience of being "lifted," inspired, made to see things in the immediate presence of God is not beyond us. Each of us has had a time when God came near, the dullness fell away from our faces and they shone; we were "lifted."

II. Connected, 17:3-4.

What came clear to every Jew who read this text is veiled from us. Moses and Elijah? What were they doing there? Every Jew would catch the significance of their presence. And I am sure this text had more meaning for the early church than it has for us.

Was Jesus an interloper, a pretender, a charlatan, a fraud? This text speaks to the question. "The Transfiguration" connects Jesus to the powerful Old Testament figures who defined the Hebrew religious experience. For us that connection is clear. The church has been telling us all of our lives that the New Testament (and Jesus) are the fulfillment of the Old. But that was not clear in the first, second, third centuries. In fact, the claim that Jesus was connected to Moses and Elijah was debated and argued and disclaimed for a long time. Moses and Elijah were rejected by the Hebrews, but God vindicated them (see *The New Interpreter's Bible,* vol. 8, 363).

Moses and Elijah were "representative" of the best and highest in Hebrew life. Moses embodied the Torah, the Law. Elijah did not leave written text, but he was primary and best among the prophetic tradition. Moses and Elijah were larger than life. They were almost too big to die. Both were taken of God straight to heaven.

"Suddenly there appeared to them Moses and Elijah, talking with him" (Mt 17:3). Jesus was not a pretender who wanted to borrow credibility from Moses and Elijah. He was fulfillment of all they did. He "talked" with them.

He was one with them. Moses, Elijah, Jesus: All were a part of the larger, redemptive purposes of God. Jesus was not an add-on to "the Law and the prophets." Jesus was completion of all Moses and Elijah came to do. In fact, their work would not have been complete apart from the life, death and resurrection of Jesus.

Too many of the people who come to church have a scatter-brained view of the Bible. They will say they "believe it." But they haven't a clue as to the plot line of it. One of the by-products of my writing and your teaching ought to be "connecting" the several stories our people know into a cohesive story. The Bible is not just a collection of stories. Those stories are saying one great message. "The Transfiguration" connected Jesus to all that had gone before in Hebrew religious history. That's why the preacher sometimes preaches from the Old Testament even though we are not Jews. Christianity grew out of, emerged from Hebrew/Jewish religion. We don't reject Abraham, Moses, David, and Elijah as we do the writings of the Koran. We connect them, blend them, feed them into our understandings of Jesus…who is the "author and finisher of our faith."

III. Confirmed, 17:5.

I believe in the divinity of Jesus. He was Messiah, Son of God and our Savior. But Jesus was just as human as he was divine. This point is about the humanity of Jesus.

The closing verses of Matthew 16 tell of Jesus preparing his disciples for the cross (see Mt 16:21-26). Jesus knew the cross was before him. And I believe he dreaded the cross. What was the Garden of Gethsemane about if Jesus did not pull back from the cross (see Mt 26:36-46)? How could Jesus be fully human and not flinch before the agony and horror of the cross?

One way to look at "The Transfiguration" is to see the whole event as God's confirmation of Jesus before he "set his face toward Jerusalem. So, Jesus stands on a mountain. His dearest disciples are around him Moses and Elijah are "talking with him" (Mt 17:3b). Into this surreal setting two "confirmations" come upon the troubled Christ:

(1) *"Suddenly a bright cloud overshadowed them, and from the cloud a voice said…"* (Mt 17:5a). Remember Moses and his leadership of the Hebrews in the Wilderness? It was a cloud that gave evidence of God's leading (see Ex. 13:21-22 and 34:5). William Barclay says, "All through the Old Testament there is this picture of the cloud, in which was the mysterious glory of God" (Barclay, *The Gospel of Matthew,* vol. 2 [Philadelphia: Westminster Press, 1958], 177). As Jesus stood in the cloud surely he could

feel the Presence of God. God was leading toward Jerusalem, and though the way was sure to be hard, he did not go alone. He went in the will of God. He was confirmed that he was on the right track.

(2) *From out of that cloud came a voice saying, "This is my Son, the Beloved; with him I am well pleased; listen to him!"* (Mt 17:5b). Jesus had heard those words before. They were exactly the words he heard at his baptism (see Mt 3:17). But that must have seemed a long, long time ago. Was he still in the Will of God? Did he still have the blessing of God? And then "The Transfiguration." He was confirmed. A long time ago when Calvary loomed before his Son, God came near and encouraged, confirmed. God still does that for all his children.

IV. Identified, 17:6-7.

Few passages in the Gospels are so crisp, clear in the way they identify Jesus. Unless you are prepared to cut "The Transfiguration" out of your New Testament, you are going to have a hard time holding to the idea that Jesus was just a religious genius or a great teacher. He was more. Much more.

And so the text takes us to the last idea we have to consider if we are to tell "The Transfiguration" story: When the disciples heard this (God's confirmation and blessing of Jesus as Son of God), they fell to the ground and were overcome by fear. But Jesus came and touched them, saying, "Get up and do not be afraid." And when they looked up, they saw no one except Jesus himself alone (Mt 17:6-7).

Moses and Elijah fade away. They have done their part in God's larger design. Frightened disciples and Jesus: They are the only ones left standing. And the text specifically says, "they saw no one except Jesus himself alone." All the attention was focused on Jesus. "The heavenly visitors depart, but Jesus stays—Jesus alone. Without heavenly companions, without heavenly glory, he is the tabernacle, the reality of God's abiding presence with us" (*The New Interpreter's Bible,* vol. 8, 364). And that's all we need. Jesus alone.

The clear message of the Gospels is this: All God had said before in Moses and the prophets was not enough. The word did not get through. But in Jesus God penetrated the barrier between heaven and earth, between the divine and the human. "The word became flesh and lived among us" (Jn 1:14). Jesus was a higher, clearer revelation of God. So, when we look to Jesus, we see God as clearly as God can be seen in this lifetime. John's Gospel was written to identify Jesus, and in one passage that is especially memorable, John tells us how Jesus described himself: "Whoever has seen me has seen the Father. How can you say, 'Show us the Father'? Do you not believe that I am in the Father and the Father is in me?" (Jn 14:9-10). But it is not John alone who "identifies" Jesus as very Son of God, Messiah, Savior. Matthew was more subtle, and in ways every Jew would recognize, he identified Jesus in the way he told the story of "The Transfiguration." I trust the long-term effect of my writing and your teaching/study will be to identify Jesus. We can have no higher service.

Conclusion

I've organized my thoughts on this passage around four words: lifted, connected, confirmed and identified. Each is in the text. Each would make an excellent lesson alone. But if I were in your place, I would not teach just a part of the text. It is rich and full. Teach as much as you can. Now bring your thoughts, mingle them with mine and build your lesson.

How Often Should I Forgive?

Matthew 18:21

ORIGINALLY PUBLISHED OCTOBER 13, 1996

Introduction

How often should I forgive? The answer is simple. Jesus said to forgive without limit. "Not seventy times, but I tell you, seventy-seven times" (v. 22). But if you read verses 15-35, you will get a larger picture—and a more complex one. I will wrestle with the real question the early church was facing and a question that still troubles the church today.

The people who made up the early church were not all saints or heroes. They were not all apostles, nor were they clones of the apostle Paul. They were just people. And because they were just people, saved by grace but still flesh and blood like you and me, they did not always get along. Members of the Christian community sinned. Sometimes when these people sinned, they were not repentant. They just kept on sinning. Sometimes the sins broke fellowship and hurt folks, and no effort at reconciliation or restoration would amend bad conduct. What then? Now we are beginning to see the problem that prompted Peter's question, "Lord, if another member of the church sins against me, how often should I forgive?" (v. 21).

One way the modern church deals with sin in the membership is to offer forgiveness automatically. We just don't deal with church discipline anymore. You can't find a self-respecting church that will discipline a member for anything. An alcoholic can refuse to take responsibility for her life; we forgive. A minister can take advantage of his office and commit sexual sin while doing pastoral counseling; we forgive. A husband can abuse his wife; we turn away.

A child can beg for her parents' love and time and get nothing; we overlook the plea. On and on this sort of turning away from church discipline goes.

Refusing to deal with sin in the congregation under the guise of quick forgiveness is not church. It is flight from the kind of life that should be present in the congregation. We are called to care for each other. We are called to high living. We are called to model relationships that attract to the faith. So we have to deal with sin in the house. Peter's question must be asked by the modern church. What do we do with people who don't meet the standard?

I. A Formula for Making Wrongs Right, 18:15-20.

"If another member of the church sins against you" (v. 15a), what do you do? Jesus recommended the following:

(1) In private, go to the offending party. State the problem. "Go and point out the fault when the two of you are alone" (v. 15b). Hopefully, this will have a happy effect. The offending party may see the problem, be sorry for the pain, and promise to make wrongs right. If this happens, you have not only corrected "the fault," you have "regained that one" (v. 15c). The fellowship of the congregation is kept intact while holy living is enlarged.

(2) Suppose step one fails. What then? Get "one or two others" to go with you. Make a second visit. Discuss the "fault" in the presence of witnesses. Hopefully, this enlarged company will accomplish what a private visit did not. Again, the goal is an end to disruptive conduct and a restoration of Christian fellowship.

(3) "If the member refuses to listen to them [the witnesses who joined you], tell it to the church" (v. 17a). Note the unwritten assumption. The congregation is the final authority for determining right and wrong for the membership: "If the offender refuses to listen even to the church" (v. 17b). When we come into church membership, we give ourselves over to the discipline of the congregation. This is not often spoken in today's church. We come in, but we reserve the right to "do our own thing." The early church did not know such individualism and would have had no part in it. Be careful to read the text. The member does not submit to the authority of the pastor; it is the congregation that has the power to correct, censor, or discipline.

(4) The congregation can exclude the member who will not allow forgiveness to happen. "Let such a one be to you as a Gentile and a tax collector" (v. 17b). This is hard for us to hear. We can recount the times Jesus welcomed Gentiles and tax collectors. But there is a difference. The tax collectors Jesus gathered to faith were eager to change and open to the gospel. The Gentiles welcomed to faith were ready to change sinful lives. We are

dealing with stubborn, unrepentant folks here. Real church has never been an "anything goes" company. When we make it so, we are not biblical. We are soft-headed, calling it forgiveness.

(5) "Truly I tell you, whatever you bind on earth will be bound in heaven, and whatever you loose on earth will be loosed in heaven" (v. 18). This is the right setting for "binding and loosing." It is not Peter who binds and looses; it is the congregation. And when the Bible is opened, and when the Spirit is called for a helper, and when earnest, caring Christians think and pray, then the will of God can be done in a hard situation with a difficult member.

(6) And Jesus will be present when the sorting out is done. "For where two or three are gathered in my name, I am there among them" (v. 20). This puts the heartwarming assurance of Jesus in proper setting. He is with the people of God when they are forced to deal with an unrepentant member of the congregation, when forgiveness can't come because the member will not let it.

II. A Principle for Standard Use, 18:21-22.

After dealing with the specific question, "If another member of the church sins against you," Peter put the question to Jesus again. "Lord, if another member of the church sins against me, how often should I forgive? As many as seven times?" (v. 21). The rabbis had said to forgive four times. Peter was more generous than orthodoxy when he suggested seven times. But Jesus took the idea further.

Wounded, broken, angry, bitter Christians are a sorry exhibition for our faith. Getting past such was the goal. And to get past a church member who is distracted from worship by the member who "sins against me," Jesus gave a principle. The principle is the basic, primary rule for all church conflict. We are to forgive. We are to forgive when it is hard, when we don't want to, when there is any chance the brokenness in Christian fellowship can be healed.

I remember a sixty-year-old man in Asheville, North Carolina. I heard him sing at a funeral. He did a good job. I asked him where he went to church, for I was new in the community. He told me he was a member of my church. I asked him if he sang in the choir. He said once he did, but not anymore. There had been a falling out in choir some time ago. He had dropped out and not gone back.

I later inquired at the church about the "falling out" in the choir. I assumed it was recent. Not so. I went to Asheville in 1964. The "falling out" happened in 1938. I had a hard time finding anyone who could tell me what the quarrel was about, but the man with the lovely tenor voice remembered. He would not forget or forgive. A God-given talent was kept from church service for most of an adult life. Why? Someone did not follow the principle Jesus gave us. To make wrongs right, the gifted man would have to begin a conversation that would let forgiveness begin. Someone has to start. It has to begin like this: "I'm sorry. Is there any way we could start over again?" Or, "It matters to me that we be friends. Can we find a way to get past the ugly and hard things that have been said? I want to be your friend."

Paul said, "Put away from you all bitterness and wrath and anger and wrangling and slander, together with all malice, and be kind to one another, tenderhearted, forgiving one another, as God in Christ has forgiven you" (Eph 4:31-32). This is the idea; this is the principle. Unless there is strong reason not to forgive, then do it. Unless the offender is hurting people and bringing embarrassment to the church, forgive. Go out of your way to forgive.

III. An Illustration of Forgiveness, 18:23-35.

Jesus made up a story to illustrate his point. "The kingdom of heaven may be compared to a king who wished to settle accounts with his slaves. When he began the reckoning, one who owed him ten thousand talents was brought to him" (Mt 18:23-24a). The story unfolds. Here are the parts I see in the story:

(1) God is "a king." We are the slaves.

(2) Everybody is in debt to the king in some way. None has a clean slate. It is not a matter of "do you owe the king?" Rather, it is a matter of "how much do you owe the king?" Put in terms we know better, "There is no distinction, since all have sinned and fall short of the glory of God" (Rom 3:22b-23a).

(3) The first "slave" owed the king a ridiculous sum. The footnote in the NRSV reads like this: "A talent was worth more than fifteen years' wages of a laborer." This man owed "ten thousand talents" (Mt 18:24). He was in so deep, he couldn't work his way out.

(4) The poor fellow begged for mercy and got it. "And out of pity for him, the lord of that slave released him and forgave him the debt" (v. 27). This is God's way.

(5) Then the forgiven fellow went out and found a "fellow slave," and he asked/demanded the man pay him the "hundred denarii" owed him. The denarius "was the usual day's wage for a laborer" (NRSV [Nashville: Thomas Nelson, 1989], 28 NT). The man who owed 100 denarii begged for time

and mercy. None was given. The poor fellow was put in debtor's prison because he could not come up with 100 denarii, but the man who put him in jail had been forgiven a king's ransom

(6) Word of this meanness reached the king. The king was angry and called the wicked slave to stand before him. Hear the king's words: "You wicked slave! I forgave you all that debt because you pleaded with me. Should you not have had mercy on your fellow slave, as I had mercy on you?" (vv. 32a-33). The king punished the wicked slave severely (v. 34). The teaching: "So my heavenly Father will also do to every one of you, if you do not forgive your brother or sister from your heart" (v. 35).

Any grievance we have between each other is small compared to the debt we all have with God. God has given us much. We ought to be able to get past, forget, find it in our hearts to forgive each other the small offenses that separate us. Since we are trying to be the children of God, why not act like our heavenly parent?

Conclusion

It is easy to say to forgive. But some sins are so socially damaging, it is hard to forgive. Battered wives will hear this word. Abused children will know what this means. Most of our differences are not of such magnitude. Try to clear out the little stuff, the underbrush that clutters our fellowship. When the sins are great, struggle to forgive. Carried grievance will eat away the soul, destroy the beautiful. When sins are devastating to the fellowship of a congregation, the congregation is empowered to act, to bind and loose.

In a Parent's Shadow

Matthew 20:20-23

ORIGINALLY PUBLISHED MAY 12, 1996

Introduction

Today's text does not give us much information about the way a husband ought to treat his wife or about the way a wife should treat her husband. We will not get a "how to" book about rearing children. Family is in this text, but it is family defined in a different way. If we sign on with Jesus, we become a part of a group. Who gets honor? How do they get it? Who gives honor? When will it come? This text is a gold mine. It is short and seems out-of-the-way, almost a digression. But when we finish, I think you will see what I mean.

I. Ambition and Politics in the Apostles, 20:20-21.

The Bible is a terribly honest book. King David is hung out to dry. We see him, sin and all. The New Testament is the same. Apostles are not put forward as models wearing halos. Their humanity is out for all to see. This text does not put them in a favorable light. They look like greedy, ambitious camp followers of a politician, and they want the best rewards for their service.

In several places, we catch a tiny glimpse of what the disciples thought they were doing when they followed Jesus. And it was not what we teach at Sunday school…at first. What they hoped for and thought they were getting was a political leader who would bring glory, and perhaps independence, to the Jews. Hints of this expectation are in Matthew 20:31 and 21:9. It is late in the ministry of Jesus. He is nearing the cross. Still there lingers in the minds of those who knew him best the hope that Jesus would be an earthly ruler and set up a Jewish kingdom in Jerusalem. This idea was not confined to the sons of Zebedee, James and John, and their mother. "A dispute also arose among them (all the disciples) as to which one of them was to be regarded as the greatest…" (Lk 22:24). So, be careful how you tar James and John. They were wrong, but they were not alone. Ambition and consciousness of place were near the surface in the apostles, and it looks like the virus infected them all.

Two thousand years is a long time. Church history now fills volumes. The story is occasionally heroic, but too often ambition and greed and pettiness still debase the glorious story of Jesus. We are saved, but sometimes it appears we are barely saved. The old ways of "me first" are at church. And "me first" was in the apostles from the beginning.

II. Mother Intervenes, 20:20.

Compare Mark 10:35-37 with Matthew 20:20-21. Note that in the Mark text the mother of the sons is not mentioned. William Barclay makes this comment on the difference in the two texts:

> The reason for the change is this—Matthew was writing twenty-five years later than Mark; by that time a kind of halo of sanctity and saintliness had become attached to the disciples. Matthew did not wish to show James and John guilty of worldly ambition, and so he puts the request into the mouth of their mother rather than themselves. (Barclay, *The Gospel of Matthew*, vol. 2 [Philadelphia: Westminster Press, 1958], 252)

I do not know that Barclay is right. He may be. And I do not know why Mark has the sons asking for themselves and Matthew has the mother asking.

Another piece of this puzzle comes of the speculation that James and John were cousins of Jesus. This idea takes root in the collection of women who were watching Jesus die at the cross. "Meanwhile, standing near the cross of Jesus were his mother, and his mother's sister…" (Jn 19-25). It has been inferred from this text that the sister of Mary was the mother of James and John. So, Jesus was a cousin to these two men. Most Bible scholars do not put much stock in this theory.

The reason I mention this is obvious: If Jesus were kin to James and John, and if the mother of James and John were the sister of Mary, then the woman who approaches Jesus in our text would be his aunt. She could presume to ask a favor of her nephew. I come at this request of a mother another way. Rather than ponder why Matthew and Mark tell a different story or try to link the woman to Jesus as his aunt, I think we are dealing with the ambition most parents have for their children. If there were favors to be dispensed, she wanted those favors to go to her boys. In the minds of these people , the new and radical nature of Kingdom service was not yet clear. The spoils system had always been the rule. They wanted their share of the recognition and honor. It was as simple as that.

III. What is "the Cup"? 20:22a.

At this point, Jesus turns the mother's request from raw ambition to the larger purpose. He would redefine what Kingdom service is really like.

(1) First, *"You do not know what you are asking"* (Mt 20:22a). I suspect Christ would say of many of our prayers, "You do not know what you are asking." And we don't. It has not been long since a young pastor asked me to help him get his name before a large, prestigious church. I know a little about that church. It has been troubled for years. No pastor of that church in the last thirty years has enjoyed the assignment. Some have worked to move from it. And I thought to myself, "This fellow does not know what he is asking." Now if I have that much information about what something sought is likely to be, how much more insight has Christ himself? Again and again the Scriptures remind us that following Jesus and attaining a place in his Kingdom will involve pain, suffering, abuse, rejection...just like it did for Jesus.

(2) Second, *"Are you able to drink the cup that I am about to drink?"* (Mt 20:22b). A paraphrase of this text comes out like this: "Can you pass through the dark waters of suffering through which I must pass?" (Sherman E. Johnson, *The Interpreter's Bible,* vol. 7 [New York: Abingdon Press, 1951], 495). Notice that when Jesus prayed in Gethsemane, he used the same phrase to describe his suffering. "My Father, if it is possible, let this cup pass from me, yet not what I want but what you want" (Mt 26:39). "The cup" we drink from full and earnest discipleship will involve suffering. Paul had it right. "I want to know Christ and the power of his resurrection and the sharing of his sufferings by becoming like him in his death, if somehow I may attain the resurrection from the dead" (Phil 3:10). No rose-colored glasses here. No escape from the hard things in life. Quite the opposite. Jesus knew what would come of serious discipleship—a cross. And so is the first reward of all who take Jesus seriously.

IV. The Unthought Courage of James and John, 20:22c.

Blundering, ambitious, hustling and all that…you can't keep from liking James and John. They did not have a clue about where following Jesus would lead. They were wrong to think there would come an earthly Kingdom and that Jesus would sit upon it and pass out favors to his own. All such is on the down side. But history does not see these men in their littleness. We measure them by a larger yardstick. We know what they did in the Book of Acts. They were giants. They had courage. They were leaders and pillars of the Church. We call them apostles.

One little bit of their greatness leaks through in this text. When Jesus said it was going to be harder than they knew, they did not blink. Jesus asked, " 'Are you able to drink the cup that I am about to drink?' They said to him, 'We are able' " (Mt 20:22c). You have to like these men. They were sold out to Jesus, and they are models for the way we must "sell out," too.

V. A Prediction for James and John, 20:23a.

Jesus says following him will be hard. James and John say they can take it…no matter. Then Jesus makes a prediction: "You will indeed drink my cup…" (Mt 20:23a). What does this mean?

Turn to Acts 12. "About that time, King Herod laid violent hands upon some who belonged to the church. He had James, the brother of John, killed with the sword…" (Acts 12:1-2). James drank deeply of the cup. He followed Jesus, and his discipleship cost him his life. This much is certain.

The end of John is clouded. Papias was a second-century writer. John lived a very long time…perhaps until nearly one hundred. But Papias says John died a martyr's death like his brother. At this point we are dealing in "tradition" which may or may not be true. This much we do know about John: He suffered much for his service. When he wrote the Revelation, he was on the island of Patmos. He had been banished to Patmos, exiled. This was a part of "the cup" John would drink. One brother lived a short life and was martyred for Jesus. The other brother lived a long life and suffered much. He, too, may have been martyred. This much is certain: What Jesus said came true. "You will indeed drink my cup…."

VI. God Gives Honor and Place, 20:23b.

Two ideas jump from this verse. Both are to be taken to heart.

(1) *Jesus does not claim more than is his.* "To sit at my right hand and at my left, this is not mine to grant" (Mt 20:23b). There is the possibility that this is a disclaimer about the future. Jesus does not know how things are going to turn in the future. But I think this misses the point. This statement is not about prediction; it is about judgment. And Jesus says judgment is not his. The people who sit at the right and left of Jesus will be those judged of God to be most worthy. And deciding who is a little bit worthy and who is most worthy is left in God's hands. Assigning final reward is God's work, and not even Jesus would dare speculate on who would get what.

(2) *Place is "for those for whom it has been prepared by my Father" (Mt 20:23c).* The foreknowledge of God is a mystery to the devout. This text suggests God knows and has known for a long time who would merit special recognition in the Kingdom of God. Maybe it will be James and John. They certainly "drank of the cup" of suffering in their service to Jesus. But heaven may have a surprise or two. I suspect it will.

Conclusion

What about family? Well there has been a family at work in this text. The people Jesus gathered around him became family. They were ever so human. They quarreled just like brothers. Each wanted the biggest piece of the pie. Each wanted first place in the affections of Jesus. But like children, they fussed and bickered and jostled for first place. And then they grew up. They learned to treasure each other, lean on each other, defer to each other. This mature apostle band is the one we see in the Book of Acts. Family? Yes, it is family. It is the family Jesus made of the people who followed him. We are a part of that family, too.

Jesus Enters Jerusalem

Matthew 21:1-11

ORIGINALLY PUBLISHED MARCH 31, 1996

Introduction

Take note of the time. This is the last week in the ministry of Jesus. Tension surrounded everything Jesus did. The Pharisees and chief priests had already plotted to kill him. They were enticing Judas to betray Jesus; money is offered. Every word Jesus speaks is being put under a magnifying glass. They are looking for evidence to use against him when they lay hands on him. Sometimes the disciples seem to understand the seriousness of the moment. Other times they would act like insensitive clods. Only after the resurrection would the disciples get the big picture. The pressure on Jesus was beyond my words to describe. He did not court martyrdom; he dreaded it. But Jesus knew how this was all going to turn out. By now his part in the plan of God was clear to him. "Thy will be done" was not pious talk; he would back it up during the trials and crucifixion (see Mt 26:39). This is background to the lesson.

Here is an outline. Parts of this lesson do not have obvious application to us. They are things reported by the Gospel writer; we need to know them. Further, they are critical to our understanding of what Jesus did for us to provide salvation. The first point in the text would have meant more to a Jewish audience than it will to us. But we have to remember Jesus was fulfillment of Scripture. Prophets predicted this event (and others) in the life of Jesus. Now to the outline…

I. Foretold by Prophets, 21:1-5

There is a sense in which Jesus lived his life by a script written long before he was born. He did not just "make it up as he went along." Great, insightful prophets came to an inspiration that was so high until they correctly anticipated what God was about and how God was going to work out our salvation. In the first point in our lesson, Jesus was acting out a prophecy (Zech 9:9).

Probably Jesus had arranged for a donkey to be available. Probably there were followers and friends of Jesus in Jerusalem who put their property at the disposal of Jesus. When the disciples went to get the colt, "it was all arranged." So, Jesus had the donkey. Two questions come to mind:

(1) What did Jesus mean to do by the triumphal entry into Jerusalem? What did he hope to accomplish?

(2) What was the symbolism preached in the event? What did it mean to a Jewish audience?

Authorities are divided about the intention of Jesus in the parade into Jerusalem. Here is what I think Jesus was about. Give this some thought before you teach.

(1) *Why the triumphal entry?* The Jewish nation was assembled in Jerusalem in solemn festival. The event confronted them. Jesus was harking back to Old Testament material. They were a holy nation called of God to high purpose. They were to be a priestly people. I think it was one last appeal to the highest and best in Hebrew history. He was calling them to get in touch with their history and dedicate themselves to acting out their mission. Jesus knew tradition blinded most people to his identity and mission. But he had to try. Further, Jesus was obedient to God's will. He did not have to go to Jerusalem. He could have stayed in the Galilee where it would have been much safer.

(2) *What symbolism was spoken to those who saw him?* Kings came into cities mounted on horses and surrounded by soldiers. Jesus came into Jerusalem on a donkey. He "was at pains to show that he led no movement of fanatical nationalism or armed revolt; he had chosen another way" (*The Interpreter's Bible*, vol. 7 [New York: Abingdon Press, 1951], 500-501). But it was more. The kingdom of God was altogether different from the kingdoms of this world. Every gesture, every prop, all the suggestions are saying Jesus is about the establishment of a different kind of throne. He was a king but a different kind of king. Was this peaceable king understood? Was the symbolism comprehended? Did it work? Did the people get what he was trying to

say? We're still trying to take in all he was trying to say on the day he sat on a donkey and rode into Jerusalem.

Until this day most of the Christian family would prefer a triumphal, crusading, conquering hero. We count. We are impressed by the trappings of power. We bow down before the big and the rich. The meek and the gentle are of small consequence. Jesus was more like those things we disdain. So, the entry into Jerusalem still comes hard for us. But the prophets foretold it. Jesus was always in touch with who he was and what he was supposed to do. Zechariah got it right. I hope we do.

II. Honored and Recognized, 21:6-9

Keep the story in view. The disciples got the donkey and brought him to Jesus. Outer garments were taken from their backs and put on the donkey. Jesus got on the donkey and moved toward Jerusalem (it would have been a short journey down the Mount of Olives and into the city). "A very large crowd spread their cloaks on the road" (Mt 21:8a). Then the crowd began to shout "Hosanna to the Son of David! Blessed is the one who comes in the name of the Lord! Hosanna in the highest heaven!" (Mt 21:9b).

I don't want you to miss the message in this text. A small group of people got the message. They saw Jesus for who he was. They took this moment/chance to honor Jesus. It was at some risk. Probably Pharisee informers were taking note of the people in the crowd. They were "taking names." Later this could be expensive for the saints. But let's not get lost in the detail.

The smallness of the group who followed Jesus has been impressed on us. At the trials of Jesus before the crucifixion we all remember how so many disciples just ran away. They were afraid. But this text tells a happy story. Some people got it. And this was a minor miracle. Consider all that was working to blind anyone from recognizing Jesus…

Tradition blinded them. The official religion was in the hands of the very people who were plotting to kill Jesus. And Jesus was denounced as trouble-maker at best and heretic at worst.

Fear paralyzed some who had a clue. I suspect a lot more people figured out who Jesus was than ever confessed him as Lord. Fear, pressure, intimidation from the religious establishment made them hunker down. Nicodemus opens a small window into this part of the Jewish community. He knew what was right; he was just afraid to go public. So, the people who praised Jesus on that Palm Sunday were a small, plucky sort. They did not knuckle under.

Mental and moral laziness was the state of most. To figure out who Jesus was and have the courage to stand up for him was just more trouble than most people were willing to endure. Is Jesus the Messiah? "Who knows? People have been talking about a messiah for years. I've got work to do." They are about "making a living." The mundane kept them from the high and holy. And this tribe is large then and now.

In our own time most people are not going to have a great deal of curiosity about Jesus and the things of God. They have to get about the ordinary of life. But some people still see him as he comes down the road. In the miracle of life they see the hand of God. In the honesty of a merchant they see moral order. In the order of our world they see intelligence and a Creator. In the death of a friend they look further and see intimations of immortality. On Palm Sunday they still see King Jesus who rides into our lives and asks us to honor him and lift a voice to cheer him. I pray the donkey and the mob and the busyness of ordinary living will not make me miss the parade. For Jesus comes riding into everyone's life. Most people just don't have the time or good sense (spiritual insight) to stop and cheer.

III. Division and Turmoil, 21:10-11

I've said most people did not take the time to figure out who Jesus was, and I believe this is true. But that did not mean the Palm Sunday parade was ignored. The text teaches the opposite. "When he entered Jerusalem, the whole city was in turmoil, asking 'Who is this?' " (Mt 21:10).

You will recall one of the reasons I suggested for the triumphal entry was that Jesus wanted to force some decision about himself and his ministry. The effect of the Palm Sunday parade was exactly what Jesus intended. A discussion is opened about who this man on the donkey is. "The crowds were saying, 'This is the prophet Jesus from Nazareth in Galilee' " (Mt 21:11).

What was the effect of the parade? It was precisely the effect Jesus predicted. "Do not think that I have come to bring peace to the earth; I have not come to bring peace, but a sword" (Mt 10:34). And in the Matthew 10 passage Jesus then goes on to say the division he will cause will be between a man and his father, between a mother and daughter, "one's foes will be members of one's own household" (Mt 10:36). And this pattern would continue throughout the New Testament, down the centuries and into our own time. Who is Jesus? What respect and worship should we give him? Does he get all of life and a serious commitment or does he get but a piece of us? Division and turmoil.

All of us want religion to be nice, unifying, lovely fellowship, good will, and all the other nice words. But that's not the way it was. Jesus came by on a donkey. Visiting Jews look up from their morning coffee and ask, "Who is that fellow?" A discussion begins. The discussion becomes heated. One fellow is pretty sure he is the Messiah and says so. Another couple of people are drawn to that idea but are afraid to say so. Most of the gathered Jews make him "a prophet." He is the prophet from Galilee who has done some remarkable things…maybe even miracles. But that's not all the group. A strong sentiment is expressed that Jesus is a trouble-maker who teaches contrary to the laws of Moses. And further strong language is used about him. He is corrupting the good Jews and ought to be put down. And so the conversation went that morning they had a parade in Jerusalem. I wonder if Jesus had a permit for that parade. There's where the Pharisee lawyers should have gotten him.

Something happens around the office. A few people see Jesus riding by on a donkey in the event. They say so. In fact, they use holy, sacred language to describe what has happened. It is modern language for "Hosanna to the Son of David! Blessed is the one who comes in the name of the Lord!" The discussion begins. Division and turmoil. So, most of the people in the office deduce that further religious discussion in the office is troublesome. They resolve not to have such conversation again. It is divisive. It makes turmoil. It's that fellow on the donkey again.

Teacher

Matthew 22:23-33

ORIGINALLY PUBLISHED MARCH 10, 2002

Introduction

This text is an illustration of Jesus' life work. Over the three years of his public ministry, Jesus came to be viewed as "Teacher." It was not a title lightly given. He answered hard questions. Tough critics who wished him ill tested him. But common people came to see in Jesus a friend who taught them with stories they could understand. He was caring and kind. He earned the title "Teacher." They listened to him because he helped them.

Sometimes Jesus was called "Rabbi." The title meant one who was knowledgeable about Jewish law and the Scriptures. There is not much difference between "Rabbi" and "Teacher." And, interestingly, Jesus' harshest critics were often the ones who called him Rabbi or Teacher. He was so obviously a good teacher that even people who wished him ill addressed him that way. We have examples of this pattern in our own time. Sometimes deists, who have a low view of Jesus and would never think of him as divine or Son of God," still say, "He was a great teacher." This session will take note of Jesus as teacher, but that does not mean we are skirting around or attempting to diminish by indirection the divinity of the Christ.

There are two strong themes in these sessions of which your class needs to be aware. First, they have to know something about Sadducees, about when this incident happened during Jesus' ministry, about the intent of the people who questioned Jesus, and about the tension between Pharisees and Sadducees. The second part of the session deals with the teaching of Jesus about how we will live in heaven. Be sure to keep the sequence in place. You have to explain the setting before you can make sense of the question about eternal life.

I. Necessary Background Material.

- It was late in the ministry of Jesus. He was in Jerusalem. It was the last week of his earthly life. Jesus was not an unknown figure trying to define himself. Jesus was a "problem" to the religious leadership and a hero to commoners.

- Pharisees and Sadducees were working to discredit him. They wanted to bring charges against him, and they needed the help of the common people to be successful. "Matthew has added them (the Sadducees) to show that with the Pharisees they form a united front against Jesus" (Eugene Boring, *The New Interpreter's Bible*, vol. 8 [Nashville: Abingdon Press, 1995], 421).

- Read the passages before and after our text. In Matthew 22:15-22 the Pharisees raise a question about paying taxes to Caesar. It was a question designed to entrap, not inform. Then our text is a question from Sadducees, a silly question designed to try to make Jesus look bad. In the verses following our text is still another question, this time from a Pharisee. Matthew 22:34-40 is about "the greatest commandment." This question had more content and seems to suggest a kind of grudging respect for Jesus.

Matthew has made a case by gathering the questions used by the Pharisees and Sadducees to discredit Jesus. If "the Teacher" could be made to look bad and if "the Teacher" could be disconnected from the crowds to whom he was a hero, then the door would be open for charges to be pressed against Jesus.

Some information about the Sadducees and Pharisees:
- Pharisees were a powerful group, though only about 6,000 in number. They had become a religious party after the Jews came home from Babylonian captivity. They were totally committed to keeping every part of the Law. They also believed in a doctrine of immortality. The Pharisees saw Jesus as radical, liberal, and a threat to all that was Jewish. In their view, Jesus was departing from the true faith.

- Sadducees were very few in numbers. They were wealthy and tended to be prominent Jews. Chief priests were often Sadducees. They enjoyed their position in life and were willing to collaborate with Roman government to maintain it. Greek ideas did not threaten them, but "in their Jewish belief they were traditionalists" (William Barclay, *The Gospel of Matthew*, vol. 2 [Philadelphia: Westminster Press, 1958], 304).

Important to our text was the Sadducees' view on Scripture. They only honored the first five books of the Old Testament, the Pentateuch. "They did not accept the prophets or poetical books as scripture at all" (Ibid.). There is no doctrine of immortality in the first five books of the Bible. The concept of immortality comes later in the Old Testament.

The Pharisees accepted all the Old Testament as Scripture, so they were committed to a doctrine of immortality. Sadducees did not believe there was any life after death. We know the question they posed to Jesus was not serious because they didn't even believe in immortality. They wanted to show up the Pharisees. They wanted to put Jesus in a bad light with a fickle crowd. All of the above was in play as the question was asked.

It's hard to take seriously a question put by people who are simply trying to make you look bad. But, sad to say, this was often the case with Jesus. Some of his best teaching was done in response to people who did not wish him well. That was the real world when Jesus lived, and it's not all that far removed from our world.

Keep in mind that Jesus took his critics seriously. He was able to do good work in a climate that was skewed and in the company of people who wanted him to fail. I've preached to some people who met all those standards. It's not easy, but it is the climate where the Lord's work has always been done.

II. The "Teaching," 22:23-33.

The Question

This question was about Levirite marriage. It was crafted to affirm the Law of Moses (the Torah or Pentateuch) and show the absurdity of the resurrection. Sadducees were clever.

The Law of the Levirite reads like this:

When brothers reside together, and one of them dies and has no son, the wife of the deceased shall not marry outside the family to a stranger. Her husband's brother shall go in to her, taking her in marriage...and the first-born whom she bears shall succeed to the name of the deceased brother, so that the name may not be blotted out of Israel. (Deut 25:5-6)

The intent of the Law was to secure the continuation of the family line into the future. "The Sadducees affirm the importance of the law because of its assumption that one's life continues after death only in the lives of one's descendants, not in a heavenly world following the resurrection. To die without offspring was thought to be an incomplete life" (Boring, *The New Interpreter's Bible*, vol. 8, 422).

The Answer from the Master Teacher

We have to face the fact that there is not much about life after death in the Old Testament. And there are even some passages that suggest there is no life after death (see Eccl 2 for an illustration). What little teaching there is on the subject is suggestive. The clearest teaching is probably from Job:

> For I know that my Redeemer lives, and that at the last he will stand upon the earth; and after my skin has been thus destroyed, then in my flesh I shall see God, whom I shall see on my side, and my eyes shall behold, and not another. (Job 19:25-27)

Jesus responded by accusing the Sadducees of not knowing the Scripture. "You are wrong because you know neither the scriptures" (22:29a). Jesus did not mean the Sadducees did not study the Scriptures; he meant they were incorrectly interpreting them. I like what George Buttrick said about this text: "Perhaps Jesus referred to such passages as Daniel 12:2-3. More likely he meant that the whole faith and implication of the Old Testament led to a belief in the resurrection" (*The Interpreter's Bible*, vol. 7 [New York: Abingdon Press, 1951], 521).

Bible doctrines grow. The way Abraham looked at worship was very different from the way Solomon did and altogether different from the way the Apostle Paul did. The idea of worship changed, evolved, emerged as people came to see more and more of the face of God. That process continues until this day. Forgiveness is another Bible idea that enlarged, shifted, and grew in the Bible. Old Testament people were asked to be as forgiving as New Testament people (Mt 18:23-35).

The Old Testament tells of Sheol, the place of the dead. It was the place for good and bad alike. There was neither exit nor hope. The great people of the Old Testament did not serve God with hope of life everlasting; they served God simply because it was the right thing to do. We have hope of heaven, but there are other and very good reasons to be faithful to God. Life "in the resurrection" will be different from anything we can imagine. "For in the resurrection they neither marry nor are given in marriage, but are like angels in heaven" (22:30). Boring has a helpful word here: "Life in the age to come is not a bigger and better version of this life—although categories of this life are our only means of conceptualizing it and expressing it" (*The New Interpreter's Bible*, vol. 8, 422).

The Bible tells us a little bit of what heaven is going to be like. The revelation to John is the best example. However, when we begin to try to give detail about creation, about the return of Christ, about the great judgment, about what heaven and hell are going to be like, we are on thin ice. Belief in the resurrection is tied to a firm, unwavering faith in the power of God. "You are wrong because you know neither the scriptures nor the power of God" (22:29b). Resurrection is not about theory; it is about faith in the power of God. So Jesus was teaching them and asking us to enlarge our faith in a God who keeps and transforms us in the life to come.

The Sadducees had given Jesus a riddle about life after death. The seven brothers died; all in sequence had been husband to the poor woman who had to bury seven husbands. To whom would she be married in the life to come? Look at it this way: God's transforming power can untangle the maze of our earthly relationships. God can untangle the messes we make of marriage, parenting, church, and well-intentioned service that turns out to do harm rather than good. God will make the crooked straight. If God can bring good out of the cross, God can "fix" the messes we make in life.

"I am the God of Abraham, the God of Isaac, and the God of Jacob? He is the God not of the dead, but of the living" (22:32). Jesus was confirming the word about the power of God. Sherman Johnson has a helpful word:

> It is worth remarking that when the phrase "God of Abraham, Isaac and Jacob" is used, it nearly always is for the purpose of emphasizing God's faithfulness to his promises. He who stood by the patriarchs is the God of the living and will give his servants a share in the world to come. (*The Interpreter's Bible*, vol. 7, 522-523)

I don't know how hard it will be to close my eyes and die trusting in the power of God to have something for me on the other side. But Jesus said God is watching, caring, and providing. All of us will have a chance to test ourselves. I don't want to be a Sadducee in that hour.

Looking Forward and Looking Around

Matthew 24:36-44

ORIGINALLY PUBLISHED NOVEMBER 29, 1998

Introduction

Our title suggests the lesson will be "forward looking." Since Advent usually signals Christmas is near, we do some translation and come out with something like this:

(1) Advent means Christmas is near.

(2) Christmas is the time when we celebrate the birth of Jesus.

(3) "Jesus is coming," when studied during Advent, means we are getting ready for the coming of the Christ Child. I looked in my dictionary and found "Advent" defined this way: "the coming of Christ at the incarnation" (*Webster's New Collegiate Dictionary* [Springfield MA: G. & C. Merriam Co., 1980], 17).

Are we getting ready for something that has already happened? Jesus has already been born. This text is not about the coming of Jesus as a baby born to Mary in Bethlehem. It is about Jesus coming again.

Many strange people have said many strange things about the Second Coming. Predictions have come and gone. Calculations about "when" Jesus will return have been fantastic and wrong. All this is in spite of the plain word of Jesus, "about the day and hour no one knows" (24:36). Most thoughtful preachers and lay people have backed away from the subject.

Matthew's Gospel does not back away from the Second Coming. Chapters 24 and 25 are about last things. Chapter 24 opens with a question from the disciples: "Tell us, when will this be, and what will be the sign of your coming and of the end of the age?" (24:3). A series of descriptions and signs about what is to happen at the "end of the age" and how we can live intelligently in anticipation of it follows the question. Our text comes from the "parables and monitory pictures" that alert Matthew's readers to the way they should act in anticipation of Christ's Second Coming (*The New Interpreter's Bible*, vol. 8 [Nashville: Abingdon Press, 1995], 444). We are "readers." The more "at home" we are in this world, the more this text has to say to us.

So our study is not "looking forward" to the birth of the baby Jesus in Bethlehem. This study is about another of Jesus' comings, the Second Coming.

I. Nobody Knows When, 24:36.

The disciples of Jesus probably speculated about when Jesus would return and when the Kingdom would be established. It is a normal way of thinking. Consider some of the ways we talk about when.

• When will the stock market go up or down?
• When will my team win the World Series?
• When will the kid at loose ends find himself?
• When will my old car "give up the ghost"?

In Christian circles, talk of when Jesus will come again has surfaced with almost predictable regularity. A preacher reads the "signs of the times" and comes up with a formula that calculates when the end will come. Events prove the preacher wrong, but that does not deter the next preacher from making another prediction.

Jesus warned us about trying to predict the Second Coming. He said, "But about that day and hour no one knows, neither the angels in heaven, nor the Son, but only the Father" (24:36). Since we can't predict it, some people dismiss it. This text tells us that too is a mistake. In fact, two ideas are held in tension in this lesson:

(1) Don't spend your time worrying about or trying to predict the Second Coming. Work steadily and be ready to give account about the assignments Jesus has given all his disciples.

(2) Give serious thought to the future. To make no provision for the world to come is a mistake.

II. God Has Come in History, 24:37.

"For as the days of Noah were…" (24:37a). This is a wake-up call. It is as if Jesus were saying, "You think God is remote and distant. You think that God coming and interrupting your calendar is impossible." But it's not.

(1) In Noah's time, God moved. God tired of sinful people living as if God didn't exist or was powerless. "They knew nothing until the flood came and swept them all away, so too will be the coming of the Son of Man" (24:39). Those people were oblivious to God. For them, the idea that God would break into the routine of life was out of the question. Jesus was saying that God moved in the time of Noah. Only Noah and his family knew God well enough to anticipate what was happening. Noah and his family were "Looking Forward and Looking Around."

(2) At the birth of Jesus, God moved. Most people missed it. Events at Bethlehem were "small potatoes" on the big screen. Rome or Athens was where the news was being made. Two thousand years later, Caesar, though still a figure of some consequence, shrinks in size next to Jesus. Knowledge of the baby from Bethlehem has grown until a great part of the world's population now claims him as their Lord and Savior.

God has moved twice. Noah and his family, Joseph and Mary, a few shepherds and Wise Men were "Looking Forward and Looking Around." They caught what God was doing. The rest? God came near, and they missed it.

III. Routine Can Anesthetize, 24:38-39.

Of the people who lived during the time of Noah, Jesus said, "For as in those days before the flood they were eating and drinking, marrying and giving in marriage until the day Noah entered the ark, and they knew nothing until the flood came and swept them all away…" (24:38-39). "Eating and drinking, marrying and giving in marriage" are what people do in every generation. These are the routines of life. Though cultures differ, the pattern is the same. The pattern goes on. We grow old and die. Our children grow old and die. Their children do the same. The beat goes on.

We begin to see life as a kind of cosmic metronome—beating, beating, beating. Jesus is telling us that this routine can put us to sleep. Routine can become an anesthesia. We quietly give up on the idea of God's intervening, Jesus' coming. We never renounce the faith. We just define it as duty in this world. We leave thoughts about the Second Coming unspoken.

Noah anticipated God. The rest were surprised. Noah was "Looking Forward and Looking Around." He had an eye for the sin of his time. He had a feel for God's response to it. He was useful to God and a model to us. Noah was not anesthetized by the routine of life.

IV. One Will Be Taken and One Will Be Left, 24:40-42.

Jesus paints a picture of what the end time will be like. "Two will be in the field; one will be taken and one will be left. Two women will be grinding meal together; one will be taken and one will be left" (24:40-41).

(1) This is not a "Rapture" scene. The word does not appear in the Bible. Jesus' description of the end time is straightforward. Christ will come and a Great Judgment will divide humankind. Then Eternity will begin. Some will be blessed, others will be cursed. The picture of "one will be taken and one will be left" is a way of describing judgment. A more popular picture of the same event is in Matthew 25:31-46.

(2) This is perhaps the most unnerving part of this passage: The two men in the field look alike, seem to be alike. The two women grinding at the mill look alike, seem to be alike. But when Jesus comes, that which is hidden from us will become clear: One is saved and one is lost (*The New Interpreter's Bible*, vol. 8, 446). We cannot anticipate the results of Judgment. It would seem that all who profess faith in Jesus would be saved, but some people don't follow their profession with an appropriate lifestyle. These are guesses about Judgment, and we would do well to leave Judgment to God.

(3) Matthew divides the house two ways. We like to divide everything three ways. There's your side and my side and then there's a middle position that is probably nearer the truth than either of "our" positions. But Matthew is not familiar with modern systems of moral grading. With amazing consistency, he tells of wise and foolish, faithful and evil, sheep and goats.

So what happens to our black, white, plus gray? It's not in the text. Somehow God is going to take into account the good in bad people and the bad in good people and come out with a two-way division of the house. I don't understand it, but this is true to Matthew's text.

V. The Call to Be Ready, 24:43-44.

The text ends where it began. "About that day and hour no one knows..." (24:36a). Then "if the owner of the house had known in what part of the night the thief was coming..." (24:43). We get this message: We can't time it. But we may miss this one: The Second Coming will be when we don't expect it.

Jesus used an illustration that I've had a hard time comprehending. He compares his Second Coming to the coming of a thief in the night. The illustration is obvious: If we knew when the thief was coming, then we would intercept the thief. But in the thief's favor is our not knowing when or where he is going to strike. It's a strange way to think, but Jesus often used illustrations that stretched the minds of his audience. So what do we get from the thief story? The Second Coming will be at a time we least expect, "Therefore you...must be ready, for the Son of Man is coming at an unexpected hour" (24:44).

How do I stay ready for the Second Coming of Christ? The question is not answered plainly until the very end of the two chapters on Last Things. Carefully read Matthew 25:31-46. According to Matthew, what will count at Judgment is the way we have acted toward hurting, helpless, needy people. Amazingly, a profession of faith is not mentioned. Do not take this text in isolation and build a doctrine of salvation on it. But to forget this text in a doctrine of salvation would do violence to the Scriptures and the clear warning of Jesus as recorded by Matthew. Paul's theology in Romans (especially chapters 3-6) needs to be put alongside Matthew's theology in our text. The combination of the two gives balance.

Risk Your Gifts

Matthew 25:14-30

ORIGINALLY PUBLISHED JULY 23, 2000

Introduction

I was a student for a long time—in fact, until I was 28. During my high school days, I didn't have to study very hard. So I didn't. But when I got to college I had to learn how to go to school, which involved two things: learning to master the material, of course, but perhaps even more important, learning to please my teachers. After all, when it comes down to it, that's really how you make "good grades."

When I came out of the army, I began to take college seriously. I wanted to know what was expected of me on tests, reports, and papers. Early on, while I thought my work to be rather good, I learned that many of my teachers had a different opinion. So I had to be willing to learn, to change. I had to learn to "think like a teacher." Many of you who have undergone the same process know that this is by no means easy. Often I wanted to quarrel with "the system," but soon realized this would get me nowhere. Once I submitted to the rules and regulations set before me, I actually began to do well.

In the Scripture for today's session, Jesus recounts a story about the rules of life. Built into our text are some abrasive ideas that are not popular. Usually we just leave these out when we study this passage, but I am going to hold them up for you to see. Most of us come from what I like to call the "Sunday School Picnic School of Theology." We want everyone to get a prize, to win at games, and ultimately, to go home happy. And the mistake we make lies in our trying to do church the same way. This could be a lovely theology, but it is just not biblical. When church is done right, believers are pushed to be honest with each other as well as themselves.

Now, that does not give us license to be hard, but it does give us a chance to tell people what God expects of us. If I wander through life aimlessly without meeting God's expectations, judgment is going to be a cruel surprise, and sadly, there will be no time to amend my ways. Often Jesus began his sermons, "Then the kingdom of heaven will be like this..." (Mt 25:1a). Jesus was telling us how to meet God's expectations. So let's listen.

I. Entrusting, 25:14-15.

"For it is as if a man, going on a journey, summoned his slaves and entrusted his property to them; to one he gave five talents, to another two, to another one, to each according to his ability" (25:14-15).

(1) The man who is going on a trip is the "God figure" in our story, and the people who work for him are called his "slaves." Though this term has harsh connotations, the mention of slavery appears frequently throughout the New Testament. God is over and above us, and we are God's servants. Paul described redemption this way: "Now that you have been freed from sin and enslaved to God, the advantage you get is sanctification. The end is eternal life" (Rom 6:22). We begin to think like Jesus when we understand that we have no control over our lives, but rather, that God is "lord over us." While this idea goes against everything our culture teaches, it is at the heart of the way Jesus perceived himself: servant to God, ready to do the will of God.

(2) Though God is lord over us, God also has confidence in us. The text explains that the master "entrusted his property" to his slaves. God uses people. Remember Abraham, Moses, the prophets, the apostles? Only rarely in the Bible does God act alone, apart from a person. Somebody is usually called to speak for God. In this particular narrative, servants are trusted to take care of and enlarge the worth of the owner while the owner is absent. By the same token, Christians at their best are about this same agenda.

(3) God does not give all believers the same qualities. Some of us are entrusted with five talents, others two, and still others only one. We would prefer that God treat everyone the same, and in a sense, God does. In Acts, Peter comes to the understanding that "God shows no partiality" (Acts 10:34). Everybody is precious to God, but that doesn't mean God gives all of us the same kind or number of "talents."

My friend Donald Jarvis immediately comes to mind. Donald was the valedictorian of my class and was always just obviously smarter than the rest of us. Did that mean the rest of us could do nothing? Not at all, but we were not nearly so gifted as Donald. That's just the way life works. If the individual who receives two talents wastes too much time fussing about not getting five, that person will not have time to multiply what they do have.

II. Multiplying, 25:16-18.

"The one who had received the five talents went off at once and traded with them, and made five more talents. In the same way, the one who had the two talents made two more talents. But the one who had received the one talent went off and dug a hole in the ground…" (25:16-18). I've preached about this parable numerous times, but I'm not sure I always get the point across. Jesus is telling us that the purpose of life is to multiply, enlarge, improve upon what God has entrusted to us.

There are plenty of churches that have "gone to seed" on multiplying, making their primary goal to get bigger faster. And when the mission of the Church is reduced to gaining numbers, clearly there is distortion. Some churches even deliberately ignore certain parts of the Gospel out of fear that these passages might push people away. But we need to hear the message: by focusing more on enlarging our congregations than we do on enlarging what belongs to God, we are failing to live up to God's expectations. Our work is to enlarge the things that are God's.

Life comes with a guaranteed built-in uncertainty factor. We don't know when we are going to be held accountable for our lives. This is where the urgency comes in. Remember Jesus' words: "We must work the works of him who sent me while it is day; night is coming when no one can work" (Jn 9:4).

III. Rewarding, 25:19-28.

"After a long time the master of those slaves came and settled accounts with them" (25:19). Most people live as if their time can be negotiated. Many are foolish enough to think they can put off "settling accounts." Even I must admit that I've gone through much of my life without giving any thought to mortality. I used to think I could play basketball with the boys at the YMCA forever. But that time has passed. I thought I could work hard indefinitely, but my endurance has weakened over time. I once thought dying was something other folks did; now my body whispers to me that I am getting old. Sometime, not too long in the future, "the master" is going to come and settle accounts with me.

Usually we devote most of our time talking about the fellow who buried his talent in the backyard and did nothing. It's quite easy to pass over the real rewards the other two servants received.

(1) God notices good work: "Well done, good and trustworthy slave" (25:21 and 23). Having had a long history of being in charge of people, I know just as well as anyone else that it is often easier to notice a person's faults than their good work. But we must keep in mind that God, who evaluates us so much more fairly than I ever could, is quick to praise and reward.

(2) God rewards good work with even greater responsibility: "You have been trustworthy in a few things, I will put you in charge of many things; enter into the joy of your master" (25:21 and 23b). Taken one way, you could conclude that God rewards good work with a lot more work. And to some extent, that is not far from the truth. But remember how you were when you were a youngster, always seeking to be more trusted, to be given greater responsibility. Deep down, most people long for more opportunities to show what they can do.

And then there is the part about the lazy, unproductive servant, who "dug a hole in the ground and hid his master's money" (25:18b). When you were unprepared in school, more than likely you dreaded facing the teacher. Similarly, I suspect the third slave hoped that the master would just decide never to come back. But he did.

(1) As we learn from the passage, the lazy servant knew a good bit about the master: "I knew that you were a harsh man, reaping where you did not sow, and gathering where you did not scatter seed" (25:24b). This fellow did not misread or fail to understand the expectations of his master. On the contrary, he knew he was expected to perform, but he simply didn't. Ignorance was not this fellow's problem.

(2) In this story, people receive different talents; however, they are equally rewarded for good work. Exactly the same words used to bless the slave who worked with five talents are directed at the servant who worked with two. Considering this, we have every reason to believe the servant who received one talent would have been blessed in the same way had he performed. The implication is that God expects everyone to try, to risk, to invest, and to work hard.

(3) Not using what you have been given is an offense to God. God expects a return on the investment made in us. What worse tragedy is there than a wasted life? When I read about kids who have already been ruined by drugs, I wonder how God will measure them. When I see people withhold

real talents from Christian service, I am fearful of the judgment that awaits them. God has put a lot into each of us and wants to see some results.

(4) What little the poor fellow had was taken from him and given to the other: "So take the talent from him, and give it to the one with the ten talents" (25:28). The teaching couldn't be more blatant: if we don't use it, we will lose it. But that is not the end of the story. "As for this worthless slave, throw him into the outer darkness..." (25:30). He didn't use what he had been given for the glory of God, and the consequences were serious.

Conclusion

"To all those who have, more will be given, and they will have an abundance; but from those who have nothing, even what they have will be taken away" (25:29). Before you trudge onward, back up and consider the way you would run a business. Surely you would tend to promote the productive employees and trust them with even more. You also would reward them for their usefulness. But the employees who don't "produce" would be slowly removed. No business can afford to carry people who don't get the job done.

We have no trouble at all hearing the grace of the gospel, but we are not so quick to hear today's story. Instead, we tend to draw back from its demands. Knowing when to press the ideas and concepts set forth by this parable, as opposed to recognizing when to back off and apply other teachings of Jesus instead, takes a wisdom that is often beyond me. But both approaches are mentioned in the Gospels. In this parable, not everybody is a winner. Not everybody gets the same number of talents. Not everyone got grace when he did not perform. The lack of performance can get you into trouble both in this world and in the hereafter. "Use it or lose it" is not just a quip—it is a biblical idea that has sharp edges.

The Table Is Set

Matthew 26:17-30

ORIGINALLY PUBLISHED NOVEMBER 2, 2003

Introduction

The subject is "Christians and Hunger." The text is Matthew 26:17-30. The setting for Matthew 26:17-30 is this:

(1) It was Passover in Jerusalem. The city was crowded with Jewish pilgrims. Since the Passover meal had to be eaten in the city (not outside the walls), "inhabitants of the city were obligated to open their houses to the visiting worshipers" (Frank Stagg, *The Broadman Bible Commentary*, vol. 8 [Nashville: Broadman Press, 1969], 29).

(2) The Passover lamb was killed at the temple in the afternoon; the meat was taken to a home and prepared. It was roasted with bitter herbs; bread and wine were then added. The room where it was served had to be free of any trace of yeast. Jesus made no reference to lamb or herbs. Only bread and wine were mentioned. None of the Jewish language associated with the Passover meal is cited in the text. This does not mean the meal did not begin as a Passover; it does mean the purpose of the meal for the church lies in another direction.

(3) The lamb was killed at mid-afternoon, served after sundown, and lasted several hours, perhaps until midnight. The people reclined as they ate.

(4) Two things happened during the meal; the second is far more important than the first.

- Jesus identified Judas as the betrayer.
- Jesus instituted the Lord's Supper for the church.

For a long time, theologians have debated about the Lord's Supper. Note Christians' different names for it: the Lord's Supper, Communion, the Sacrament, the Eucharist, and the Covenant. During the Reformation, a contentious dialogue developed about what the Supper means, who could take it, and who could administer it. Those old arguments still entangle our thinking. We are not truly interested in old arguments. We want to know what the text says. What does it mean? I will try to answer those questions. Three ideas need to be emphasized.

I. Christ's Death and the Forgiveness of Sin, 26:26-29.

"While they were eating, Jesus took a loaf of bread, and after blessing it he broke it, gave it to the disciples, and said, 'Take, eat; this is my body.' Then he took a cup, and after giving thanks he gave it to them, saying, 'Drink from it, all of you; for this is my blood of the covenant, which is poured out for many for the forgiveness of sins. I tell you, I will never again drink of this fruit of the vine until that day when I drink it new with you in my Father's kingdom' " (26:26-29).

Here is what I think these profound verses mean:

(1) *The symbols point to the cross.* We would pay little attention to broken bread and "poured out" wine if they were not joined to the cross. The symbols were acted out. What Jesus did in drama on Thursday night he did in deed on Friday morning. This text tells us just how intentional Jesus was about the cross. The cross had to be. The church is making a statement: the death of Jesus was/is at the center of our gospel.

(2) *The sacrifice had meaning.* "Jesus took...bread...broke it, gave it to the disciples, and said, 'Take, eat; this is my body' " (26:26). Bread gives nourishment. It sustains us and allows us to live and work. It is not eaten for pleasure, bread is required for life. The death of Jesus gives life and strength to all who believe. Evil did not prevail at the cross. In the giving of Jesus' life, we were given life everlasting.

(3) *The point of it all was forgiveness of sins.* Eugene Boring said it well: "The whole action is related to the forgiveness of sins.... The forgiveness of sins is Jesus' primary mission" (*The New Interpreter's Bible*, vol. 8 [Nashville: Abingdon Press, 1995], 471). William Barclay put it this way: "Jesus claimed to be the great liberator. He came to liberate men from fear and from sin" (*The Gospel of Matthew*, vol. 2 [Philadelphia: Westminster Press, 1958], 377). Sometimes we wander from first principles. We emphasize ideas that

are derivative rather than primary. The Christian religion begins with forgiveness of sin; the cross put forgiveness within reach.

(4) The Supper has a future tense: "I tell you, I will never again drink of this fruit of the vine until that day when I drink it new with you in my Father's kingdom" (26:29). Every Lord's Supper anticipates another time and place. There will come a day when Eden's damage will be undone; salvation (now in process) will be complete. Christ will gird himself and serve us. We will have no need of symbols; the resurrected Christ will host the meal.

II. Self-examination Is Part of the Supper, 26:20-25.

Jesus identified Judas as the one who would betray him, but he did it in an indirect way. The effect of the announcement caused all the disciples to ponder whether they were the guilty party: " 'Truly I tell you, one of you will betray me.' And they became greatly distressed and began to say to him one after another, 'Surely not I, Lord?' " (26:21b-22). Does this part of the text merely convey historical data (Jesus knew Judas was the one who was going to betray him)? If that were the case, we could skip these verses; they are fact, but not teaching. But I believe there is more.

(1) The earliest record of the Lord's Supper is in 1 Corinthians (see 1 Cor 11:17-34). Paul made self-examination a prominent part of a spiritual inventory that each participant should take: "Whoever, therefore, eats the bread and drinks the cup of the Lord in an unworthy manner will be answerable for the body and blood of the Lord. Examine yourselves, and only then eat of the bread and drink of the cup" (1 Cor 11:27-28). A flippant state of mind has no place at the Lord's Supper.

(2) Now let us compare Paul's injunction to "examine yourselves" with our text. When Jesus suggested he knew who would betray him, each disciple examined himself. Jesus could have said, "Judas, you think you are sneaking around in your conversations with the priests, but I know what you are doing. You have sold me for thirty pieces of silver." Had he done that, the other disciples would have prevented Judas from fulfilling his agreement with the priests. Jesus let Judas know and let him free to do his wickedness. An indirect result of his approach afforded all the disciples a moment of self-examination and perhaps self-doubt.

(3) None of us is as calculating and cold as Judas, but all of us have compromised our profession of faith in little ways. We have been less than we promised when we first professed faith in Jesus. The Lord's Supper offers us a time to take our spiritual temperature. We need to reexamine regularly our profession of faith. When the disciples broke the bread and took the cup

together, they were renewed. The communion was with Christ and the people of Christ, and they went out from worship with strength and with each other. Our communion with others grows out of our communion with Jesus.

The church has recorded the Lord's Supper with great care. Four times it is described in the New Testament (Mt 26:26-30; Mk 14:22-25; Lk 22:14-23; 1 Cor 11:23-34). The conviction of the church is that what happened in Jerusalem the night before Jesus died created a new covenant between God and God's people. My study Bible has a title page introducing the New Testament that contains these words: "THE NEW COVENANT COMMONLY CALLED THE NEW TESTAMENT OF OUR LORD AND SAVIOR JESUS CHRIST."

Usually we pass over the title page. Not today. Our text explains the choice of words on that page. What Jesus did at that first Lord's Supper made a new covenant between God and a people, the church universal. Blood sealed the covenant God made with the Hebrews. The blood of Christ sealed the covenant we have with God today. John Broadus summarized, "Our eating and drinking these (the bread and wine) symbolize our personal union with Christ and feeding our spiritual nature upon him" (*Commentary on The Gospel of Matthew*, 531). Remember the symbol: We have swallowed a bit of bread symbolizing the body of Christ. He is in us, with us; we have fed upon him and drawn our strength from him. So Paul would write the Colossians of a great mystery: "Christ in you, the hope of glory" (1:27b).

John Calvin interpreted the Lord's Supper to mean Christ meets us at the table each time we gather. He did not hold to a literal meaning of "This is my body," but he believed that every time we take the Supper, Christ is there. The first meaning of "communion" is the presence of the resurrected Christ when we take the Supper. We commune with him as we feed upon him. But there is more.

Evidently the Gospels provide only a skeletal account of all Jesus said that night. Paul sheds more light in 1 Corinthians 11:23-26 (most people agree that Paul received much of his instruction from Peter). Jesus quietly turned a Passover meal into the Lord's Supper. With time, the early church evolved and expanded the Supper and made it a part of regular worship. Almost certainly it became a time when Christians pledged their love, loyalty, and life to Jesus. It was built into the Sunday service and repeated regularly. They believed there was core gospel in the Supper, so when they observed it they were giving a witness: "For as often as you eat this bread and drink from the cup, you proclaim the Lord's death until he comes" (1 Cor 11:26).

Years passed. Persecution came to the early church. Staying with Christ and the church became risky. Those who stood near when promises were made and the bread and wine were taken became closer than brothers and sisters. A shared commitment to Christ, a shared risk for Christ, and a shared purpose in ministry—all came together. When they took bread and wine, they were no longer isolated, alone, and afraid. When they broke the bread and took the cup together, they were revived and made strong. The communion was with Christ and the people of Christ, and they exited worship with strength and with each other. Our communion with each other grows out of our communion with Jesus. The one is primary; the other is derivative. Both are exceedingly important.

What does this text and teaching have to do with Christians and hunger? This text is about feeding humankind's greatest hunger. When Jesus said, "Take, eat; this is my body," he was offering soul food (pardon the pun). There is evidence that Jesus cared for sick bodies, hungry bodies. Yet Jesus never forgot that we are body and spirit. The food offered in the Supper is for our deepest need; it will sustain us to life everlasting.

Churches are divided. One group insists that the gospel is about salvation and sin, faith and grace, judgment and heaven. The other group of churches touches lightly on the ancient ideas cited above; they hurry to themes like hunger, race, war, ecology. This text starts us in the right place. We begin by feeding at the deepest level. The hunger for forgiveness of sin and for reconciliation with God is addressed in the Lord's Supper. We feed on the body and blood of Christ and are made strong to be Christ's people in a new company called the church.

Suffering Servant

Matthew 27:32-66

ORIGINALLY PUBLISHED MARCH 24, 2002

Introduction

For us, the problem with the crucifixion is that we know Easter is coming. This knowledge steals the terror from the event and robs it of reality. We know Jesus is not going to stay in the tomb. We know "everything's going to work out all right." This session will have life and power if you can help your folks get back in touch with what the cross was like. There was an awful day when the cross was real and Easter seemed an eternity away, much like what we are experiencing in these days. I want to recreate that day, and I want to find hope in the cross…even before Easter.

The accounts of the trial and death of Jesus are not identical. The variations add detail and give us additional glimpses of what Calvary was like. No Gospel is more vivid, stark, and plain than Matthew. He does not shield us from the pain. Manners and "good form" often trump truth. There is none of that in Matthew. God's way of "saving the world" was not pretty nor did it meet the standards of the fastidious. As a baby Jesus was born in a manger around cows and sheep, so the death of Jesus was done with nails in his hands, enemies taunting, and friends at a distance or gone. By the time we get to Paul's letter to the Romans, the church has processed what happened, seen the hand of God in the agony, and come to "glory in the cross." Here's what I think is important in our session: The early church remembered the dying. The early church remembered Easter. We do well when we claim both. This session emphasizes the grim part, but that does not make it a "downer."

There was a long journey toward Jerusalem. Jesus told the disciples what was coming. In Jerusalem Jesus and his friends celebrated Passover, went out to Gethsemane, and prayed; Judas found him, kissed him, and the trials began.

I. Pain.

I have rarely taken apart piece by piece the events of Calvary. Most of the time I reference that Jesus died on the cross and move on. Our text forces you and me to take a close, hard look at a gruesome sight. Most of us don't want to get too close to Calvary. Crucifixion was a slow death, calculated terror, and pain. Crosses were commonplace in the Roman world. It was Roman capital punishment, and Romans were not squeamish about imposing it.

I'm not sure any of us can speak with certainty about the state of mind of Jesus as he died. Jesus was more than we are. Jesus was on a mission and connected to God in ways beyond my understanding. So if I speak of what Jesus was thinking, I am at the edge, and you need to beware of that. Jesus died a humiliating, agonizing death, and we need to look at it. His friends and enemies misunderstood him. If you read the charges brought against Jesus by the religious establishment, you realize they are partly true. His friends did not understand that he would really die, although Jesus warned them repeatedly. "Jesus began to show his disciples that he must go to Jerusalem…and be killed, and on the third day be raised. And Peter took him aside and began to rebuke him" (Mt 16:21-22). The disciples misunderstood.

Jesus' enemies misunderstood him in a different kind of way. "You who would destroy the temple and build it in three days, save yourself! If you are the Son of God, come down from the cross" (27:40). Jesus had made those claims, and for us they have become the building blocks for our theology, but Jesus' enemies heard these truths as blasphemous. It is hard to work for three years to explain yourself but still be misunderstood.

Jesus was made public sport; he was humiliated and stripped. Soldiers cast lots for his clothes (27:35). With sheer cruelty, Jesus was taunted: "He saved others; he cannot save himself. He is King of Israel; let him come down from the cross now, and we will believe in him" (27:42). Where were the people who shouted, "Hosanna to the Son of David! Blessed is the one who comes in the name of the Lord!" (21:9)?

The sense of abandonment is overpowering. Matthew does not report even one disciple at the cross. John puts himself there (Jn 19:25-27), but the other Gospels tell that Jesus was abandoned by his friends. Dying alone, separated from the people who know you best, has to be special pain. The apostles become heroes in the book of Acts, but they were cowards at Calvary.

The text suggests Jesus felt abandoned by God. "And at three o'clock Jesus cried with a loud voice, 'Eli, Eli, lema sabachthani?' " [that is, 'My God, my God, why have you forsaken me?'] (27:46). Jesus was quoting Psalm 22:1. George Buttrick says, "Was Jesus in the depth of despair, or was he meditating on the words of Psalm 22 in confidence in God's victory? To that we can make no dogmatic answer, for plainly we do not know" (*The Interpreter's Bible*, vol. 7 [New York: Abingdon Press, 1951], 608). Eugene Boring gives some relief to an otherwise bleak statement, "The human Jesus is pictured as dying with a cry of anguish and abandonment on his lips, and yet not of despair. In the darkness and pain, he still addresses his lament to God, as 'my God'" (*The New Interpreter's Bible*, vol. 8 [Nashville: Abingdon Press, 1995], 492).

There are times when the present is so hard and so cruel until all of us wonder where God is. In the moment, Jesus was somewhere between the larger purposes of God and his own agony. He cried out for relief as he did in the garden of Gethsemane. Jesus had to struggle through Calvary for you and me, and the record is clear: He felt he was alone. I don't want to die alone, and Jesus didn't either. It was hard.

II. Hope.

Some of you will see this point as "reaching." That is, I'm going beyond the text to impose my interpretation. Maybe I am, but there is a Bible idea that supports what I am doing. In the darkest days of Hebrew history, when prophets were scolding and predicting doom, those same prophets always found some way to say that there would come a day when things would get better. Christians die in hope. We grieve as we lay away our dear ones, but we grieve in hope (1 Thess 4:13). The gloom that surrounds this session is deep and pervasive. There needs to be a word of hope. You check and see if the text will support me.

The natural order noticed. After he "breathed his last," Matthew tells us, "The earth shook, and the rocks were split. The tombs also were opened, and many bodies of the saints who had fallen asleep were raised" (27:50-52). Of the earthquake and premature resurrections, Buttrick wrote, "God wrote in darkened sky and torn mountains his judgment on our wickedness, and his love for Christ" (*The Interpreter's Bible*, vol. 7, 609). Even nature has a conscience, and when awful things happen, nature mourns. Pagans began to rethink who Jesus was. "Now when the centurion and those with him, who were keeping watch over Jesus, saw the earthquake and what took place, they were terrified and said, 'Truly this man was God's Son!' " (27:54). Notice how Matthew weaves into the story the continuing debate about who Jesus was. Our theme for this session is from the beginning. "Who Is This Jesus?" was on the mind of Roman soldiers who were assigned the ugly task of executing a crucifixion. Something about the way Jesus died gave a witness and raised a question in their minds. The centurion's exclamation at Jesus' dying was not a full-blown affirmation in Jesus, but it was a beginning. The church would build on it.

Not all of Jesus' friends abandoned him. "Many women were also there, looking on from a distance, they had followed Jesus from Galilee and had provided for him. Among them were Mary Magdalene, and Mary the mother of James and Joseph, and the mother of the sons of Zebedee" (27:55-56). Two comments: First, recording the presence of the women put the apostles in a bad light. Women were there; apostles weren't. Scripture is true, and sometimes truth hurts. Second, it may be that the women told Peter, Mark, Matthew, and Luke what we know of the cross. They were there. And though pain must have dimmed his vision, Jesus had to notice the only people at the cross who truly cared for and understood him. The people who crucified Jesus were not sure they had done away with him. "Chief priests and Pharisees gathered before Pilate and said, 'Sir, we remember what that impostor said while he was still alive, "After three days I will rise again" ' " (27:62-63). Those people hated Jesus and saw to it that he was killed, but they had been listening to what he said.

They heard what Jesus said when he predicted resurrection, and they knew he was larger than life. They anticipated the Easter event though they dreaded it. From the perspective of 2,000 years there is almost humor in the closing lines of our text: "Pilate said to them, 'You have a guard of soldiers; go, make it as secure as you can.' So they went with the guard and made the tomb secure by sealing the stone" (27:65-66). As if their guard were going to restrain Easter!

III. History.

We will teach this session too small if we stick only to the assigned text. The larger message is in Acts and Romans, in 1 Peter and Revelation. If I put my nose close to the page and tell just what is in Matthew 27:32-66, I will almost misrepresent the event described in those verses. This text cries out for a larger interpretation. It is not just what happened at Calvary. We need to move on to the larger question: What does it mean?

The church wrestled for 300 years to "explain" Calvary. The Apostle Paul marked the way:

> While we were still weak, at the right time Christ died for the ungodly. Indeed, rarely will anyone die for a righteous person.... But God proves his love for us in that while we still were sinners Christ died for us. Much more surely then, now that we have been justified by his blood, will we be saved through him from the wrath of God. (Rom 5:6-9)

Roman Catholics, Greek Orthodox, and Episcopalians never go to church without celebrating the Lord's Supper. It is so central to their understanding of who Jesus is and what worship is until they keep the cross and dying of Jesus ever before their people. Great cathedrals are built in the shape of a cross. Priests wear crosses. Churches have crosses on their steeples. The cross marks, defines, and bears witness to the central event in God's great expression of love—the gift of his dear Son to save us from our sins. Let's not forget the "big picture." It tells us what Calvary means and who Jesus is.

The Resurrected Lord

Matthew 28:1-15

ORIGINALLY PUBLISHED MARCH 31, 2002

Introduction

We meet the same problem with Easter that we had with the cross. We've heard the story before. The story doesn't hold our attention, for we all know how the story ends. Knowing the ending should not dull our effort. Easter and resurrection are not just central pieces to our theology; they are also central to the way we process things as personal as the death of loved ones and our own aging.

Easter and resurrection are foundation pieces of a Christian worldview. Quietly, almost by stealth, the idea that this world is all there is creeps back into our culture. It is modern paganism. If there is a place for religion, it must be a religion of the "here and now." In a sense it is revival of Deism. There is a God, but that God is remote. Jesus was a great ethical teacher, but the Jesus of miracle and resurrection is not emphasized. Rule and right conduct, mercy and helping the helpless are becoming the foundation pieces of a new understanding of what it means to be Christian. We teach this kind of gospel indirectly. For example, we almost never mention resurrection in a Sunday sermon, we rarely discuss immortality except at funerals, and the traditional doctrines of Christianity are marginalized. Instead, we stress missions and helping. We lift high the obligation to feed and house. We've become "this world" people, and we've reshaped our gospel to fit our revamped worldview.

Now a disclaimer: I believe in missions to the hungry and helpless. We have a peculiar obligation to share, help, lift, feed, heal, and teach. These good works are an extension of the ministry of Jesus. But what is amiss is the silence about Easter. When I was a graduate student at Princeton Theological Seminary, Chad Walsh came to our campus. In an address to seminarians, Walsh asked if we lived in a one or a two-story house. What he meant was this: Did we really believe there was life after death? We live on the ground floor of life in this world, but over and above this world is another world (so he called it a two-story house). Walsh delivered his addresses to us in 1955. That was a long time ago, but he was on to something. He saw that we were drifting from some basic ideas that had always been central to our faith. Today, I live on the ground floor that is this world. Because of the resurrection, I hope to move upstairs at my dying. I have hope and faith in Jesus; therefore, I believe the resurrection that came to Jesus will in God's good time come to all who believe in Jesus (see 1 Cor 15). To live with eternity in view is to be Christian. To have a hope that reaches beyond this world and into the next is being Christian. The foundation of that hope is Jesus. God raised Jesus from death and because Jesus lives, I go about my life with a different frame of mind. I am on mission with a gospel of hope…in short, everything is changed.

I. The Mood Changed.

I know of no more somber, grim literature than Matthew 26–27. The betrayal, trials, and crucifixion of Jesus are heavy beyond my words to describe. But with Matthew 28:1 everything changes. "And suddenly there was a great earthquake; for an angel of the Lord, descending from heaven, came and rolled back the stone and sat on it…. The angel said to the women, 'Do not be afraid; I know that you are looking for Jesus who was crucified. He is not here; for he has been raised' " (28:2-6a). Nature had honored the dead; there was an earthquake while Jesus hung on the cross. Now there is a joyous shaking. Goodness has prevailed in spite of all evil could do.

From this point forward in the New Testament, there is a joy, a brightness, in everything. Of course there is joy in the resurrection accounts, but it goes further. Luke describes the church right after Pentecost like this: "Day by day, as they spent much time together in the temple, they broke bread at home and ate their food with glad and generous hearts, praising God and having the goodwill of all the people" (Acts 2:46-47a). Joy became the Christian style. Paul wrote the Philippians, "Rejoice in the Lord always; again I will say Rejoice" (Phil 4:4). Jesus is alive. He sustains us in life and prepares a place for us in death. Our joy began with the resurrection.

II. God Acts.

Throughout the trials and crucifixion of Jesus, God stood aside and allowed wicked people to plot, seize, and kill Jesus. Where was God? Worse still, was God unable to "do anything"? These are the kinds of questions that surface any time there is great tragedy. During the Holocaust, where was God? During the horror of Stalingrad, where was God? During the genocide in Yugoslavia, where was God? And sometimes in ways too personal to recite, our dear ones suffer and slip away, and where is God?

I can't answer all the questions life presents, but I can lift high our text to say that God is alive and aware. The God who stood aside during those agonizing hours on the cross is the same God who stepped up on Easter.

God led the early church by the torch that was the Holy Spirit. It was the Spirit that took control at Pentecost. The Spirit is another face for God. Today, the same Spirit that gave Pentecost gives light and life to my church and yours. For over 2,000 years that flame has brightened the darkest night. God has been inside the church directing, reforming, redeeming, and refreshing. God continues to act, and it all began on Easter morning.

III. Understandings Changed.

This idea is implied in our text, but there is no shortage of New Testament base for it. Jesus would often give a teaching that the disciples would not understand. Matthew 16 illustrates the point. On a retreat when Jesus and the disciples were apart from the pressure of the crowds, Jesus asks the Twelve: "Who do people say that the Son of Man is?" They gave several answers. Then Jesus became more direct: " 'But who do you say that I am?' You are the Messiah, the Son of the living God.' And Jesus answered him, 'Blessed are you, Simon son of Jonah!' " (16:13-17). Then Jesus began to tell them that he would go to Jerusalem, suffer, and die. At that point Simon Peter, the same man who had such insight just moments before, said, "God forbid it, Lord! This must never happen to you" (16:22b). Truly, Simon Peter did not really understand until after Easter. The disciples did not take in the messianic and salvation parts of the Gospels until after Easter. They had seen enough and comprehended enough to stay with him during his life, but the real plot line of Scripture would not come clear to them until after Easter. Sometimes I question the insights of the disciples. Why didn't they "get it"? But in more tolerant and rational moments I realize that I'm more like them than I like to admit.

Easter was a watershed for the church. We don't know all the mind of God. Like Paul, we still "see through a glass darkly" (1 Cor 13:12 KJV). But now we understand more than before. Easter made clear the plan of God.

IV. The Identity of Jesus Changed.

When the disciples saw the resurrected Christ, they acted differently. "Suddenly Jesus met them and said, 'Greetings!' And they came to him, took hold of his feet, and worshiped him" (28:9). I think this is a critical moment in the Christian religion. In a sense the resurrected Jesus was the same person he had been before. In a deeper sense he was profoundly changed in the eyes of the church. Two quotations help to make my point:

> The resurrection is not merely the happy ending of an almost-tragic story of Jesus, a postscript at the end. The resurrection perspective permeates the story throughout, so that all of Matthew's story is testimony to the risen Lord of the church. The resurrection is thus to be preached from all twenty-eight chapters, not only from the last…. Without the resurrection, the whole story evaporates. (Eugene Boring, *The New Interpreter's Bible*, vol. 8 [Nashville: Abingdon Press, 1995], 505)

> Before Easter Jesus was "prophet" or "Messiah."…After Easter all the old titles became too small—tiny nets that could not sweep an ocean. After Easter Jesus was "Lord," "the Word," "our Savior." That event turned their blindness into piercing sight, their earthly ambition into love of the brotherhood, their cowardice into courage that feared no persecution or death. The Resurrection is the great divide in human history. (George Buttrick, *The Interpreter's Bible*, vol. 7 [New York: Abingdon Press, 1951], 619)

Our theme has been raising the question "Who Is This Jesus?" The truth is that you can't get a grip on this question apart from Easter and resurrection. To answer the Jesus question, you have to get on the Christian side of Easter. Jesus is our friend, indeed, but that's not all there is to it. We worship the Christ we see in Easter glory. We gather on Sunday, the first day of the week, the day Jesus was resurrected—an Easter people in worship around a resurrected Christ.

V. After Easter We Became a People on Mission.

Our session would end with parts dangling if we did not sneak a peek at the end of the chapter. Much Jesus had said to his disciples before, they now understand. Resurrection took their blinders off. Four things take place so quickly we can miss them:

(1) *Worship.* "When they saw him, they worshiped him; but some doubted" (28:17). This repeats what happened on Easter morning (see 28:9b). Jesus is friendly, but he is also awesome, glorious, the aura of heaven surrounding him. He is worthy of worship.

(2) *Empowered.* "All authority in heaven and on earth has been given to me" (28:18). Some of that authority was given to the disciples being sent on mission. Mission work is hard. If there is none of the Lord, if some of that resurrection energy is not given, then mission work is too hard. Jesus knew that and equipped his people for mission.

(3) *Commissioned.* "Go therefore and make disciples of all nations" (28:19a). When first these fisherman followed Jesus there was a promise: "Follow me, and I will make you fish for people" (Mt 4:19). Now that promise was being kept. They had a new job. The Gospel writers tell of the commissioning in different ways (Mk 16:15; Lk 24:45-49; Jn 20:21-23), but none omits when Jesus set them to task.

(4) *Presence.* "And remember, I am with you always, to the end of the age" (28:20b). Jesus gave power and promised that we would not be alone when we do his work.

Jesus came to this earth on mission. When he left this earth he set his own on mission. We are successors to the apostles. We have not had all the experiences of the apostles, but we are in a line that extends from those apostles. Their work is ours to do. If we catch the vision of Easter, if we can truly see the resurrected Christ, then we will be fit to see the job through. More than any other session, this one answers the theme question: "Who Is This Jesus?"

A Directive for Missions

Matthew 28:16-20

ORIGINALLY PUBLISHED JULY 7, 1996

Introduction

Saint Paul told us "all scripture is inspired by God," and we try to take all the Bible seriously (2 Tim 3:16a). But not all Scripture has had the influence of today's text. When you step back from the immediate and try to see the Christian movement in perspective, what you see is truly amazing. Let me show you what I mean....

The place is a backwater of the Roman Empire. Over in little Judea, a troublesome place, there is a disturbance. Established religion is challenged by an itinerant preacher. The establishment bribes, begs, and bullies. The itinerant preacher is killed. And that is that.

Well not quite. The most unlikely story emerges. The itinerant preacher comes back to life. He gathers his pitiful little band of followers around him. He tells them they are to go everywhere and "make disciples." The followers were not promising; in fact not one of them seemed capable of real leadership. The itinerant preacher disappeared. The followers said, "He went back to heaven." And then the followers began to go from house to house, from town to town, from country to country, from continent to continent. And less that three hundred years later the Roman Empire called herself "Christian," and worshiped the itinerant preacher, calling him Savior and Lord.

Why did the followers go from house to house, from country to country? What made them do it? What drove them to "go and tell"? This lesson gives the reason.

Before getting into a verse by verse explanation of what I see in this text, I want to reinforce this text. I will work from the Matthew statement of the Great Commission. But Luke, John, and Paul all tell us of the same thing. After Jesus was resurrected, the disciples were assembled and a command was given to go and "make disciples." What we are studying today is not standing on a slender scriptural base. Rather, all the Gospels save Mark give us a Great Commission. The life of Paul is a living testimony to missions. He was truly the greatest of all Christian missionaries. So, today we are working from one text, but we are studying the sense of the New Testament.

I. The Setting, 28:16-17.

Lose the setting and you lose much of the power in this text. This was not just any meeting between Jesus and the disciples. I suspect all the disciples saw at least a little part of the crucifixion. It was a terrible scene. And when you have on the cross someone you love and have followed for three years and someone in whom you had bet your life and put all your hopes…then the crucifixion must have been devastating beyond my words to describe. The disciples did not have any trouble believing Jesus had been killed; they had trouble believing he was resurrected. They knew he was dead.

Now two women (see Mt 28:1-10) come and tell them to go to Galilee to a place Jesus had told them to assemble before he was crucified (see Mt 28:16). They do this, and Jesus meets them there.

By Matthew's account, none of the disciples has seen the risen Lord. This is a first resurrection appearance. "When they saw him, they worshiped him" (Mt 28:17a). Prior to the crucifixion they had not "worshiped" Jesus (see Mt 14:33 for an exception). The Greek for worship means they threw themselves on the ground before him. The crucifixion/resurrection of Jesus completed the identification of Jesus as Savior and Lord. He was worthy of worship.

"But some doubted" is present from the beginning (Mt 28:17b). We can suppose this would include Thomas; John's Gospel gives more detail about this "doubt" (see Jn 20:24-29). I like George Buttrick's comment on "some doubted." "Doubt is perhaps not the opposite of faith, but only faith's misgiving. We could hardly doubt what does not exist. If we doubt God, we have perhaps therefore already glimpsed him….There is faith in honest doubt" (*The Interpreter's Bible*, vol. 7 [New York: Abingdon Press, 1951], 621). Don't be too hard on the disciples and their doubt. I would have had a hard time taking in the resurrection, too. For the disciples, it was simply incredible! The command to "go and tell" was a kind of last will and testament.

II. The Authority, 28:18.

The text reads, "And Jesus came and said to them, 'All authority in heaven and on earth has been given to me' " (Mt 28:18). It is as if the Messiah/Lord of the Church no longer hides himself in a manger as at birth. No longer does this Lord of life put on the humility of a street preacher. Now he takes up the symbols of his majesty and commands.

But back to authority. "All authority" meant the right to appoint to office. Jesus would share some of his authority with the appointed. In John's Gospel we get the Great Commission in a different form. " 'As the Father has sent me, so I send you.' When he had said this, he breathed on them and said to them, 'Receive the Holy Spirit. If you forgive the sins of any, they are forgiven them; if you retain the sins of any, they are retained' " (Jn 20:21-23). This authority the Church has mishandled on occasion, but that the authority was given is not in doubt.

Baptists have taken texts like these and made them large. We readily ascribe to Jesus full authority. It is the other people and the other offices and the other institutions we want to limit. To get people to answer to Christ alone is the goal. To get people to enthrone Jesus Christ, crucified and risen is what we seek. To limit the authority of a pastor—and when you consider some of the things pastors have done—makes good sense. A pastor serves under the authority of a calling from the Lord and a calling from a congregation. Both must be honored. A denominational authority is foreign to the New Testament. Apostles are no longer among us. No office we have created should claim or exercise authority over a congregation. The Christian religion is not just anything. It is life under authority...the authority of Christ himself. And like the apostles, all of us need to fall down and worship him.

III. The Commission, 28:19-20a

This all-important text breaks into three parts:

(1) *The command:* "Go therefore and make disciples..." (Mt 28:19a). An assignment was given. The disciples were to become the carriers, ambassadors, evangels, and missionaries. The purpose in the going was to "make disciples."

We live in a time of shallow, half-thought religion. Often you will hear the glib comment: "One religion is as good as another." If it were, the Great Commission would not have been given. There is truth in other religions, but George Buttrick put it this way; "They are the flush in the sky before the dawn. But Christ is the brightness of his rising... (*Interpreter's Bible*, vol. 7,

622). We go because people without Christ are lost, separated from God and in need of the Good News of Jesus Christ.

Take into account the way the disciples heard the command to "go and make disciples." They broke free of the bonds of Judaism; it was hard for them to do. But they broke free and went around the Roman world. Paul made one missionary journey after another. The Early Church sent her best to the furthermost places. And everywhere they went, there sprang up believers and churches. So until this day we imitate those first disciples. We go and tell. I have the pure delight of working for an organization that spends the largest part of our income doing exactly what Jesus commanded us to do. We are in the "going and telling" business. This text is our Bible base.

(2) *The scope:* "Make disciples of all nations." In little lines here and there in the Gospels you will see Jesus broadening the scope of the Kingdom. Greeks want to see him in John 12. The Syro-Phoenician woman was his care. But now it is lined out. "Make disciples of all nations."

And so "one world," a phrase so put down by some politicians, is actually good Bible interpretation. God loves Communist children just as much as he loves ours. God loves Muslim children as he loves ours. God loves all his children, and he commands us to go to the ends of the earth to reach all his estranged, separated children. And our real brothers and sisters in eternity will not be determined politically; rather, the real kinship will be a common Savior. And all who say his Name and hold high his cross are kin to me.

(3) *The means:* "Baptizing them…teaching them…" The way we "make disciples" is to baptize them and teach them.

"Baptizing them in the name of the Father and of the Son and of the Holy Spirit" is more profound than we know. To baptize one "in the name of…" means "to baptize into the possession and protection of the Godhead, and to establish a vital union between God and the believer" (Sherman Johnson, *The Interpreter's Bible,* vol. 7, 624). When I am baptized, I literally belong to Christ. I am in the care of the Godhead. I am no longer my own. I am bound over into the keeping and service of Another.

IV. The Promise, 28:20b.

"And remember, I am with you always, to the end of the age" (Mt 28:20b). Jesus was sending them into unknown, hostile territory. The life and death fate of the disciples was frightening. The coming of the Holy Spirit as the Presence was still in the future. It would take fully as much faith to do what Jesus has told the disciples to do (go and "make disciples") as it would to believe in the resurrected Christ.

I have read several missionary biographies. David Livingston said when he was most alone in parts of Africa not yet on the map, there Christ was with him. Buttrick quoted James Gilmour, missionary to Mongolia, who said, "No one who does not go away, leaving all and going alone, can feel the force of this promise" (*Interpreter's Bible,* vol. 7, 625). My life is small potatoes when compared to such courageous missionaries, but when I have risked the most, I have been nearest the Presence. Jesus kept his promise.

So much of our Christian faith is kept, safe. So little is risked, at peril. When we get into the tight places, the dangerous places, those are the times when the Presence comes close, and we know Jesus is near. C. S. Lewis has a seven-volume series of stories for children. The God-figure in these stories is called Aslan. Aslan is a lion. Aslan is not on every page of *The Chronicles of Narnia.* Only when the children are at risk in their adventures does Aslan always draw near and walk with them. So it is with us. Maybe the reason the Presence is so remote to so many is that so many are remote to the first mission of the Church.

Have You Repented?

Mark 1:1-15

ORIGINALLY PUBLISHED FEBRUARY 20, 1994

Introduction

On two counts today's lesson is going to be hard for some of your people to hear. These two counts have done great harm to our ability to hear this teaching: The street preacher shouts above the traffic, "Repent! Repent!

(1) Repent! Unless you repent you will all go straight to hell!" The people pass him by and tie repentance to radical religion. Since they are not radical about anything, they have no plan to get into radical things like repentance. Such ideas are for the crazy fringe of religion.

(2) The "New Age" guru quietly explains away any idea of guilt. In fact, we need to get out of our minds the notion that being religious passes any judgment on anyone. Judgment and repentance are a part of the language of an old and outdated way of thinking. If only we can come into the modern world we will put down all the old language that goes with guilt. Repentance is a part of the old; repentance has no place in modern religion. And there is one more idea I am hesitant to put forward. I suspect repentance is not a part of the preaching of a lot of our preachers. It is a dated word. Repentance sounds old fashioned. Preachers (and I am one) are influenced by the fads of the day. Besides, we all have faults...the preacher included. So, occasionally there is lip-service to repentance, but to tell the truth, the idea has been neglected in too many churches.

One Sunday school lesson is not going to make all wrongs right, but if done well it can be a good start. If we are going to be into biblical discipleship, we are going to have to get into repentance.

I. Religion Is Personal; Repentance Is Personal.

What's beneath this text is just as important as what the text says John the Baptizer and Jesus preached to people who had formalized their religion. A pattern both in thought and action developed over centuries. The Jews came to think that because they were Abraham's children and because they were chosen of God, they were acceptable to God. It was as simple as that. By way of inheritance I am put right with God.

Now it was understood some formalities had to accompany this inherited faith. They had to go to the temple and observe the feasts and circumcise their sons and obey some rules. All of these formalities were of the essence of Jewishness. Jews were known by the way they ate kosher foods, studied Hebrew, went to synagogue on Friday night. That was the way Jews acted. But who you are and how you get that way is determined by inheritance.

Jesus had long discussions with the Jews about the nature of true religion. John records some of these discussions. Especially instructive is John 8:39-47. Note their almost plaintive plea, "Abraham is our father" (Jn 8:39 NRSV). But Jesus was wanting more. He was looking for a personal religion. Now this formalizing of religion is not confined to the Jews. In the Middle Ages our Christian religion was reduced to a community thing. Everyone was baptized. If your parents were baptized and if you lived in a "Christian country," it was assumed you were Christian too. The Reformation tried to turn back the clock, get in touch with New Testament patterns and lead the Church to a converted membership.

Now we are the children of the Reformation. But it has been nearly five hundred years since Luther tacked his theses on the door of Wittenburg church. In great measure we have lapsed back into a formalized, ritualized religion. The children of the saints routinely became members of the Church. And in due time their children will become members, etc.

John the Baptizer and Jesus are saying that kind of ritualized religion does not cut deep enough. Religion is personal. It is not inherited. A Christian family helps; a Christian family can't guarantee. Good religion is not a gene passed from parent to child. Good religion comes upon us when each of us, one by one, repents of his/her sins and turns in faith to Christ. Both John and Jesus made much more of repentance than we do. Don't get into the idea that repentance is pentecostal, radical religion; repentance is New Testament religion preached with force and repetition by John and Jesus.

II. Religion Is Change; Repentance Is Change.

Seems to me we make the most of repentance when we bring people into the faith. So, in our traditional salvation formula we say something like this:

(1) Have you repented of your sins?

(2) Do you now believe in Jesus?

(3) Will you confess Jesus before the congregation and be baptized? If the answer to these questions is "Yes," then the candidate is voted into the congregation and baptized. Repentance is there, but repentance is not stressed beyond conversion. So, in the mind of many of our people repentance is something you do as you come into the church and that's that.

I don't doubt the sincerity of our people at their baptism. Most of the people I've baptized were very much in earnest. Some of them had some heavy sins to repent, and the weight of their sins led to remorse. Repentance led to relief. This is not where the trouble lies.

Our error in emphasis lies in defining repentance as a conversion teaching. Once we get beyond "entry level Christianity" there is little said about or little need for repentance. This is the mistake. I want you to think about the way Jesus defined repentance. It is a larger idea, a ore recurring idea than most have noticed. In rapid-fire order I am going to list some repentance themes in the teachings of Jesus. And l want you to see how they involve the total person's change:

(1) "Either make the tree good, and its fruit good; or make the tree bad, and its fruit bad; for the tree is known by its fruit" (Mt 12:33 NRSV). Religion/repentance means change.

(2) The scribes and Pharisees are condemned for cleaning "the outside of the cup and of the plate, but inside they are full of greed and self-indulgence: (Mt 23:25 NRSV). Religion/repentance mean deep personal change.

(3) What Jesus wants of us is "the second mile" and love for the enemy (See Mt 5:41-45). This is more than most of us ever explore This is serious change, and serious change is the turning from an old life and the redirection to a new life that is repentance.

(4) Stark is Jesus' demand that "none of you can become my disciple if you do not give up all your possessions" (Lk 14:33 NRSV). This is Barnabas change, repentance change.

(5) When Jesus spoke of greatness he said, "Truly I tell you, unless you change and become like children, you will never enter the kingdom of heaven" (Mt 18:3 NRSV). Here is good religion lined out and it means change. Repentance is this kind of change. It is a reorienting of life. It is a change in the way we think about all things.

I suspect some of you think I've wandered from the subject. But I hope you see the connection. Repentance is the recurring theme in the message of Jesus. It involves change in every part of life. And these changes are not accomplished in an instant. No one can really make these changes at the moment of "conversion." So, the life that is following Jesus is a life being changed. And regularly we are made to repent of our worldly ways of thinking and acting and change to the Jesus way. In each change we will repent.

III. Religion Is Constant: Repentance Is Constant.

The more we get into the Christian religion the more we are going to be aware of our sins. Only the insensitive soul who is distant from God is untroubled by sin. The nearer we come to God, the nearer we are to holiness and the more we are aware of the difference between God and ourselves. So, the saints are always troubled by their sins. Paul would call himself "Christ Jesus came into the world to save sinners—of whom I am the foremost" (1 Tim 1:15 NRSV).

What this means is that every Sunday in worship the most devout are going to be looking for a time when they can confess their sins and be forgiven. They are looking for a time to do repentance. The week has cluttered their lives. These are not gross sinners. They are subtle sinners. But the near saints know this is not worthy of the one who is following Jesus. They are looking for a time to repent and change and go a new way.

Now what happens if we do not repent of this daily accumulation of sin? We will be like a house that never carries out the garbage. We will begin to smell of old garbage. Repentance is carrying out the trash from life. It is needed on a regular basis, and if we don't have it we get in foul shape. I've heard people way, "Why do I need worship every week?" Here is the answer. And to design times for repentance and forgiveness into every worship is the assignment of those who build worship.

Conclusion

I've not given you an outline for this text as I usually do. This is not because I take the text lightly. Rather, I've consciously tried to line out for you the enormity of repentance as a theme in the preaching/teaching of Jesus. My material will be more background and shaping than usual. But this subject (repentance) seemed to me to be one that has been mishandled by us all. I've made some effort to put repentance back into the Christian life. Not just in at the "entry level." Rather, repentance needs to be a part of the way we look at all of life as we are being converted. God willing, the conversion is still happening for all. If that be so, repentance is a part of the process.

Preparing for the Good News

Mark 1:1-8

ORIGINALLY PUBLISHED DECEMBER 5, 1999

Introduction

Mark's Gospel was written earlier than the other Gospels. In fact, Matthew and Luke borrowed much of their material from Mark. William Barclay goes to some length to show that Mark is both the first as well as the source Gospel for Matthew and Luke. He concludes with this summary: "So the result is that there are only 24 verses in Mark which do not occur somewhere in Matthew and Luke" (*The Gospel of Mark* [Philadelphia: Westminster Press, 1956], xiv).

Since Mark is the source Gospel, it is important to determine Mark's source. Where did he get his information? Papias lived about a hundred years after the apostles died, and he gathered information about the earliest days of the Church. Regarding Mark's Gospel he said, "Mark, who was Peter's interpreter, wrote down accurately, though not in order, all that he recollected of what Christ had said or done" (Ibid., xvii). So when we read Mark, we are getting what Mark remembered of Peter's preaching.

I comment on sources because of the way Mark opens his Gospel. He never mentions the baby Jesus. Our text is the opening eight verses of the Gospel, and then Jesus bursts onto the scene full-grown. When he is first mentioned, John the Baptist is baptizing him (see Mk 1:9). Both Matthew and Luke devote two lengthy chapters to the announcements, birth, and honoring of the infant Jesus.

How could Mark leave out such consequential stories as those concerning Mary and Joseph, shepherds and angels, Herod, the flight into Egypt,

Simeon and Anna, the twelve-year-old Jesus in the temple? These are my ideas:

- The Early Church did not dwell on the infant Jesus.
- Jesus' ministry and teaching is more important than the implied teachings of the nativity stories.
- Mark compressed the life of Jesus. It is action-packed, fast-moving. The word he used so often was "immediately." It appears forty times in sixteen chapters. We have "the essential, no-frills added" Jesus in Mark.

Does this mean Matthew and Luke erred? Not at all. We would be impoverished had Matthew and Luke not found additional sources and added them to their Gospels. Mark contains only 661 verses. Matthew, however, had 1,068 verses, and Luke 1,149. Mark never offers us the infant Jesus. Instead, he opens with John the Baptizer, a genuine, card-carrying prophet, dressed in camel's hair and living in the wilderness of Judea. If that's the way Mark opened his Gospel, I suspect that was the flavor of Simon Peter preaching as well.

I. Jesus Identified, 1:1.

"The beginning of the good news of Jesus Christ, the Son of God" (Mk 1:1 NRSV). Actually, this is not a "verse" in any normal sense. "The first verse is probably the equivalent of what in a modern book would be the title…The verse should therefore be set off by itself, and end with a period" (Frederick C. Grant, *The Interpreter's Bible*, vol. 7 [New York: Abingdon Press, 1951], 647). Two strong and quite different ideas flow from this short verse/title:

(1) Mark tells us point-blank what he aims to do. He tells us Jesus is "the Son of God," and he does not just say it once. The message will appear again and again.
- During Jesus' baptism, a voice comes from heaven: "You are my Son, the Beloved; with you I am well pleased" (1:11).
- The demon-possessed man addressed Jesus with more insight than he realized, saying, "What have you to do with me, Jesus, Son of the Most High God?" (5:7b).
- Atop the mountain at Transfiguration, a voice speaks from a cloud, saying, "This is my Son, the Beloved, listen to him!" (9:7b).

This message reappears yet again in 14:61-62 and 15:39. Obviously, Mark is intent on telling us that Jesus is the Son of God. "Son of God" means that it is by way of Jesus that we get our best, most accurate information about God. When Philip asked Jesus to "show us the Father, and we will be satisfied," Jesus said, "Have I been with you all this time, Philip, and you still do not know me? Whoever has seen me has seen the Father" (Jn 14:8-9). Mark is clear from the start that Jesus is the Son of God.

(2) In an altogether different way, Mark says this is "the beginning of the good news of Jesus Christ…" (1:1). The previous point was reinforced in the text. This one, however, allows the imagination to run free. When Jesus came, "good news" began to move about.

- Good news: Rules and law are not the way to know or satisfy God; grace is introduced to the human family.
- Good news: Sin is not forever; it can be forgiven and "washed away." We can borrow goodness from Jesus.
- Good news: barriers, tribes, borders, languages need not divide the human family. We are "one in Christ Jesus." Trace the effects of good religion in history.

The religion of Jesus had everything to do with the war against slavery. Godly people like Dag Hammerskjold and Jimmy Carter have restrained wars. Mother Teresa and David Livingstone extended life and encouraged mercy. In fact, Livingstone opposed the slave trade in Africa until the day he died. This kind of illustration could run on and on. Morality has given order to society. Mercy has founded and funded hospitals. Education has been encouraged and bright minds have been opened—all in the name of the "good news," beginning with the coming of Jesus.

II. Jesus Connected, 1:2-3.

"As it is written in the prophet Isaiah, 'See, I am sending my messenger ahead of you, who will prepare your way; the voice of one crying out in the wilderness: 'Prepare the way of the LORD, make his paths straight' " (1:2-3). Verses 2-3 are a combination of two quotations (possibly three) from the prophets. That is the reason the King James Version reads, "As it is written in the prophets…" (1:2a). "See, I am sending my messenger ahead of you, who will prepare your way…" is from Malachi 3:1, and it is very near to Exodus 23:20. "The voice of one crying out in the wilderness: 'Prepare the way of the LORD, make his paths straight' " is from Isaiah 40:3a.

Why would Mark go back and connect Jesus to these Old Testament prophecies? For the apostles and the early Church, these "connecting" quotations from the Scripture were crucial. The Old Testament was the only Scripture to them. The New Testament was yet to be written. When Peter preached (and John Mark wrote), connecting Jesus to Jewish history and prophecy was essential. It explained who Jesus was and what he came to do. He was not a pretender, here today and gone tomorrow. Jesus was the long-awaited, predicted-by-the-prophets Son of God.

Connection meant legitimacy. So phrases like, "from the foundation of the world" appear in Matthew, John, Ephesians, Hebrews, 1 Peter, and Revelation. They are saying this: God has planned the life, death, and resurrection of Jesus for a long, long time. Jesus is the full disclosure, the completion of something God has nurtured for a long time. Mark quoted the prophets to "connect" Jesus to the larger, longer designs of God. Peter said in his first epistle, "He (Jesus) was destined before the foundation of the world, but was revealed at the end of the ages for your sake" (1 Pet 1:20). What Mark was about to say in the Gospel that bears his name had been a work in progress for a long time.

III. Jesus Introduced, 1:4-8.

"John the Baptizer" is the right name for John. John wasn't a Baptist; he was a "baptizer." John the Baptizer's mission in life, his reason for being, was to introduce Jesus. The text tells us three things about John:

(1) John started a revival of religion in the Judean wilderness. The unusual, distinguishing feature of John's revival was his baptism. It was a "baptism of repentance for the forgiveness of sins" (1:4b). Sins were labeled plainly (see Lk 3:7-14). People were convicted, repented, and in turn John baptized them to seal their new resolve to be cleaner, more godly people.

This revival was no small event. "People from the whole Judean countryside and all the people of Jerusalem were going out to him, and were baptized by him in the river Jordan, confessing their sins" (1:5). Luke tells of "priests and Levites from Jerusalem" who were sent to question John about who he was and what he was doing (Jn 1:19-28). I suspect John the Baptizer was a larger figure in Jewish life than he is in our Gospels. Throughout the ministry of Jesus there is evidence of John the Baptizer's ministry. Diggings in the Essene community, the one that has given us the Dead Sea Scrolls, suggest the ministry of John the Baptizer may tell us of a community where his disciples lived.

(2) What was John the Baptizer like? He was eccentric, a loner, a God-driven prophet cut from the mold of Elijah. His choice of the Judean wilderness for his revival is strange. It is lonesome country. It is dry and desolate, like parts of West Texas and New Mexico. His dress and his diet were peculiar.

But for all his unusual ways, he was strikingly authentic. He had to be taken seriously. People from all over sought him out. They were hungry for a religion that was "the real thing." He was so right, so honest, so selfless until people forgot how he dressed or what he ate. People listened to what he said.

John said: "The one who is more powerful than I is coming after me; I am not worthy to stoop down and untie the thong of his sandals. I have baptized you with water; but he will baptize you with the Holy Spirit" (1:7-8). "One more powerful than I" would not have made sense had John not been preaching to a throng of people. When he said, "one…more powerful than I…," the people could not take it in. After all, how could there be a preacher "more powerful" than John? He was the greatest preacher who had come to them in a long time. But in the long stretch of history John was right. John was the opening act and Jesus is the main attraction.

More important than "who is the greatest" was the very nature of what John and Jesus could do for people. John "baptized with water." It was a sign of repentance, and it was undoubtedly significant. But Jesus would "baptize…with the Holy Spirit." Jesus was able to touch and change the human heart in ways John could not. And John realized this from the start.

I recall when the vice president of the United States was coming to Asheville. I was asked to say a brief prayer at the event. Someone would get to introduce the vice president, and a few would sit at the head table at the dinner, but none of us was the feature. We all had small parts to play. John the Baptizer by himself seems of small consequence, but when you see the part he played in introducing Jesus, then you understand the place he has carved for himself in history. He lingers around the edges of the stage, because he was chosen to identify and baptize Jesus.

Now reduce the picture. None of us has been so honored as was John the Baptizer, but we can make our lives of eternal worth when we do something a little bit like John. As we introduce Jesus, we find a niche, a footnote in God's larger scheme of things. We have a part in "preparing for the good news."

Family Priorities

Mark 3:31-35

ORIGINALLY PUBLISHED MAY 5. 1996

Introduction

I am taking some liberty with my assignment. I am writing a lesson on Jesus and family. I will roam through the four Gospels finding bits and pieces here and there about the subject. One part of what I find is our text. But I am going to give you a larger Bible base for the big idea of Jesus and family.

Before I get into the lesson, let me warn you. We live in a time when family is handled badly. Women are abused in the home. Children are bred and forgotten. Too many respectable people, and often church people, have children and then hire someone else to rear them. Older women are divorced and left alone, often destitute. About half of our marriages end in divorce. Now 30 percent of American babies are born out of wedlock. Put all of this family mess in a bag and shake it up, and what you get is a national tragedy. We have made a mess of family.

Into the family mess climate comes a lesson on the family. One would think the direction would be to elevate family and make more of it. Or, make us take vows to do family right. But that is not the direction the Gospel fragments on family take us. I am going to stay close to the texts. I am going to teach what the Gospels say.

Today's text is covered in my last point. So, if you wonder what has happened to it, go to the last point. I offer you an outline on the title, Jesus and family. Use the parts that are helpful.

I. Jesus Had a Care for His Family, Mark 6:1-6. John 2:3-5, 19:25-27.

Selected texts in the Gospels can give the impression Jesus had little regard for his family. When Mary and brothers came looking for Jesus in Mark 3:31-32, and when Jesus was asked to go to them, he replied, "Who are my mother and my brothers?" (Mk 3:33). The feel of the text is that Jesus has little regard for Mary or any remnant of the family who reared him in Nazareth. I will speak directly to this text later, but I think we misread what Jesus was saying if we conclude he had little regard for his mother or his family. Here is additional insight into the way Jesus felt about them....

(1) *Jesus did not forget his hometown. He went back home.* Matthew, Mark, and Luke tell of a trip Jesus made back to Nazareth. It was not a satisfying visit, but that is not the point. Jesus did not abandon his family or his home place (see Mk 6:1-6, Mt 13:53-58, and Lk 4:16-30 for full descriptions of the trip back home).

(2) *Jesus "came through" in a difficult social situation.* In John 2:1-12, we find Jesus at a wedding. In the course of the celebration, the hosts run out of wine. Mary, the mother of Jesus, comes to him and says, "They have no wine." And Jesus said to her, "Woman, what concern is that to you and to me? My hour is not yet come." His mother said to the servants, "Do whatever he tells you" (Jn 2:3-5). It sounds as though Jesus were rude to his mother, pushing her away. But she did not take it that way. She promptly told the servants to do as he directed them. And then as Mary had expected, Jesus came through. Mary's request was honored even though Jesus had some reluctance to do what she asked.

(3) *Jesus provided for his mother at his dying.* As Jesus hung on the cross, both his mother and his aunt were near. Several Gospel texts suggest Mary was never far from the ministry of Jesus. Now Mary and her sister agonize as they watch him die. But Jesus was not caught up in his own pain. "When Jesus saw his mother and the disciple whom he loved standing beside her, he said to the disciple, 'Here is your mother.' And from that hour the disciple took her into his own home" (Jn 19:26-27).

Though there are difficult passages in the Gospels suggesting Jesus pulled away from his family, a closer study will show Jesus had a care for the family who reared him and made provision for them.

II. Jesus Did Not Order His Life Around Family, Luke 2:41-51, 9:59-60.

Early in the life of Jesus, we find an idea creeping into his mind: I am under higher authority than the authority of my mother and father. This same idea would be in his ministry.

(1) *The boy Jesus in the Temple at age twelve listens to a higher authority.* You recall the story (see Lk 2:41-49). Joseph and Mary take the twelve-year-old Jesus to Jerusalem for the Passover. When the festival was ended, Jesus did not go home with his parents. He stayed "in the temple, sitting among the teachers, listening to them and asking them questions" (Lk 2:46). He amazed them with his answers, but that is not our point. What of his family? Mary said to Jesus, "Child, why have you treated us like this? Look, your father and I have been searching for you in great anxiety" (Lk 2:48b). You can feel the care in the mother's question. The boy Jesus replied, " 'Why were you searching for me? Did you not know that I must be in my Father's house?' But they did not understand what he said to them" (Lk 2:49-50). Even the boy Jesus had figured he would march to a different drummer. He hears other voices. He was to be obedient to a Higher Authority.

(2) *Family is not highest priority.* Once on impulse a fellow offered himself to Jesus. But offering of self was conditioned: "To another he said, 'Follow me.' But he said, 'Lord, first let me go and bury my father.' But Jesus said to him, 'Let the dead bury their own dead; but as for you, go and proclaim the kingdom of God' " (Lk 9:59-60). I will not unpack all "Let me go and bury my father" means, but the point is plain—family must not order life. It is secondary to commitment to God.

I suspect there is more in this teaching than we want to hear. Most of us do family and do our religion. We try to balance the two. We try to keep the one from limiting the other. But that is not always possible. Paul would counsel the completely dedicated follower of Jesus to the single life (see 1 Cor 7:8-9). He was into a kind of commitment that would not take the time family required. For Christ's sake, some are still called to this total, single commitment. Either way, single or married, family was not the highest priority to Jesus. A total commitment to discipleship was.

III. Family Can Be an Obstacle to Serious Discipleship, Matthew 10:34-39.

This point just takes the previous one to a higher power. It is easy enough to choose the good when good and bad are put in clear, stark contrast. The hard choices come when we must choose between competing good things.

The Pilgrim's Progress is not read by our generation. In an earlier time the book was most influential on church people like you and me. John Bunyan wrote the book while in prison for preaching the gospel, between 1660 and 1672. The story is all about Pilgrim and his journey toward the Celestial City. The first test Pilgrim faced as he began the journey was the test of leaving his family. Listen to Bunyan...

> So I saw in my dream that the man began to run (beginning his journey toward discipleship and salvation.) Now he had not run far from his own door, but his wife and children perceiving it began to cry after him to return; but the man put his fingers in his ears, and ran on crying, "Life, life, eternal life." So he looked not behind him, but fled towards the middle of the plain. (Bunyan, *The Pilgrim's Progress* [Middlesex England: Penguin Books, Ltd, Harmondsworth, 1965], 41)

Bunyan has the sense of Jesus. Jesus said to his own disciples,

> Do not think that I have come to bring peace to the earth; I have not come to bring peace, but a sword. For I have come to set a man against his father, and a daughter against her mother, and a daughter-in-law against her mother-in-law; and one's foes will be members of one's own household. Whoever loves father or mother more than me is not worthy of me; and whoever loves son or daughter more than me is not worthy of me; and whoever does not take up the cross and follow me is not worthy of me. Those who find their life will lose it, and those who lose their life for my sake will find it. (Mt 10:34-39)

The same idea is found in different language in Luke 12:49-53. It is radical discipleship. Jesus was calling for a commitment that would overshadow, eclipse, and overpower all others. It is an unnatural thing to leave household, family, and dear ones. But we have such a watered-down notion of what commitment is in our churches until we usually dismiss texts like this. They make no sense to us; so we just snip them from the Scripture and ignore them. This is not the kind of discipleship Jesus asked.

For two years, my daughter was a missionary in Japan (1979–81). She taught English to Japanese. One class was directed toward college students, and out of that service came six or seven students who chose to go public with their commitments to Christ. Each of those students paid dearly for that public commitment. Their families were against what they were doing, and in some measure each of these students acted out exactly what Jesus said in the Matthew 10 passage…"one's foes will be members of one's own household." I have seen some of this rejection and tension with family right here in our own country. When high school and college people get so serious about their Christian commitments until they begin to think about ministry and missions, often American parents will counsel these young people to "be careful, you could waste your life…don't go overboard and get unbalanced in your religion." We are not as far from this idea as we like to believe. We want our children to be religious…just not too religious. So the barrier to serious discipleship becomes "members of one's own household."

IV. Family Is Redefined with Jesus, Mark 3:31-35

Today's text is the gospel base for this point. When Mary and the brothers of Jesus came to see him, Jesus did not hurry to them. And in a way that seems harsh to us, he said, " 'Who are my mother and my brothers?' And looking at those who sat around him, he said, 'Here are my mother and my brothers! Whoever does the will of God is my brother and sister and mother' " (Mk 3:34-35).

The apostle Paul would have understood this statement. It seems Paul lost his family in the service of Christ. No mention is made of them. But Paul was not without family. When he visited with the Ephesian elders on his last journey to Jerusalem, there is this text, "When he had finished speaking, he knelt down with them all and prayed. There was much weeping among them all; they embraced Paul and kissed him, grieving especially because of what he had said, that they would not see him again" (Acts 20:36-38a). Did Paul have a family? Yes. His brothers and sisters were those who did the will of God…just like Jesus said it would be.

My life has made me a wanderer so far as my parents, brother, and sister are concerned. We have not lived near them much. Our daughter did not live in a family with grandparents, aunts, uncles, and cousins near. But that did not mean we were without. In the most remarkable way, some friends in the faith/church stepped forward and became grandparents and uncles and aunts and cousins to our daughter. We were not without family; God gave us a larger and new family. And all the while we were still in touch, though miles removed, from some blood kin who are very dear to us. This Scripture has been lived out in my experience.

Then the text has another meaning. Sometimes blood kin come to a wayward or pagan life style. They do not share the Christ commitment. They do not care about the things I care about most. I am more like people to whom I am not kin than I am like people who are my blood kin. G. K. Chesterton once observed, "Ask your landlady what she believes about God. If what she believes and what you believe are near, you can probably live in that landlord's house. If not, you may not get along." Chesterton was observing that what we think about God defines us and groups us. The people who share our commitment to Christ really are "brother and sister and mother...", just like Jesus said.

Conclusion

Parts of this lesson are not "conventional wisdom." But I believe I have given you a balanced package of what Jesus believed and acted on family. You will note there is no word on how husbands and wives are to get along or on how we are to rear our children. Paul has a bit of that, and more is in the Old Testament. But this lesson is about Jesus and Family. This lesson pushes all of us toward a more serious discipleship and a rethinking of family in our own time.

The Gospel and Storytelling

Mark 4:26-32

ORIGINALLY PUBLISHED MARCH 2, 2003

Introduction

Jesus had a way with words. Several times in Mark's Gospel we see just how well he communicated.

- "He entered the synagogue and taught. They were astounded at his teaching, for he taught them as one having authority, and not as the scribes" (Mk 1:22).
- In Mark 12 Jesus refuted "the scribes," and "The large crowd was listening to him with delight" (v. 37b).
- Perhaps the strongest affirmation of his ability to communicate comes indirectly: "When Jesus saw the crowds" (Mt 5:1a), and the Sermon on the Mount follows. People wanted to hear what he had to say.

Our title is "The Gospel and Storytelling." Jesus was a master communicator. Jesus used stories to catch and hold his audience. He could take the common and use it to illustrate the profound. Parables were stories from daily life, yet they illustrated spiritual truths (ideas about the kingdom of God). And that's what this text is about.

Here are some thoughts about the Gospel of Mark that may help you as you interpret today's lesson.

(1) Mark was the first Gospel written. It was a source for Luke and Matthew.

(2) Tradition has ascribed this Gospel to John Mark, the nephew of
Barnabas and a traveling companion of Paul. John Mark actually witnessed
the ministry of Jesus. Papias lived in the second century (about 100 years
after Peter and Paul died). He gathered material about the early church.
"Papias tells us Mark's Gospel is nothing other than a record of the preaching
material of Peter" (William Barclay, *The Gospel of Mark*, [Philadelphia:
Westminster Press, 1956], xvi). I go with tradition.

(3) The basic material in Mark was circulated orally before it was written. But remember the date: around AD 70. The early church was in crisis.
And, to compound the problem, Peter and Paul had stepped off the stage.
Age and persecution had taken away the first generation of leadership. What
now? Are we going to die and is our cause going to die with us? These were
the questions on everyone's mind as this text was penned.

(4) I believe Jesus spoke these parables, but Mark focused them to the
special needs of a persecuted, frightened, unsure people. Two more ideas:

• What does "the kingdom of God" mean? Think of "the kingdom of God"
  as the rule of God. With the coming of Jesus, the "kingdom of God has
  come near" (see Mk 1:15a). The ascension of Jesus did not take away the
  kingdom of God. Jesus planted, and what he planted continues to grow.
• What is a parable? Most people who come to church have some idea of
  what parable means. It is a story that takes a familiar idea and changes the
  way we think about it. Money we know. Jesus told a story about a rich fool.
  That story puts a question in my mind about trusting in money. There are
  times when I trust in money, but the parable causes me to think differently
  (see Lk 12:13-21).

The setting for these parables influences the way I interpret them. I'm
trying to determine what Mark was saying to his original audience. We need to
know that before we can correctly know what the parable means for us. Keep
the date of writing in mind; keep the condition of the early church in mind.
They were discouraged and afraid. Mark was speaking to their condition.

I. Kingdom Seed Will Grow, 4:27.

I compared Jesus' work to a farmer planting seed. His preaching was sowing
ideas. The parables we are studying are from farm life. Most of us aren't
farmers these days, but we have gardens that grow vegetables, fruits, and
flowers. From our gardening we can connect with these parables.

Now put yourself in the place of a threatened, first-century Christian. You have joined the little band of believers. When Jesus went back to heaven, there were but "one hundred twenty persons" (Acts 1:15b). The apostles did their work, but they were growing old. Some had been put to death for their faith. Others were in prison. For all the effort of Paul, could the little churches (outposts of the kingdom of God) survive?

Jesus anticipated the need. He told a story from farm life that answers the all-important question "Can the church survive?" This parable takes the survival of the church (and kingdom) out of our hands. The parable says the seed has already been put in the ground. In a way that is mysterious, beyond our arrangement, the seed will grow.

Gardeners can do but so much. Seed germination is dimly understood even by those who make such their profession. Halford E. Luccock said, "The real point of the parable is not the gradualness of the growth of the seed, but the sureness of the growth, its inevitability" (*The Interpreter's Bible*, vol. 7 [New York: Abingdon Press, 1951], 704). This idea answers our question. The kingdom of God is going to survive because God will see to it.

The idea I've just stated can be taken to the extreme. I could reason like this: "If the seed will grow no matter what, what does it matter whether I am busy about kingdom work or not?" The parable doesn't excuse us from work. We can plant and help with the harvest. But the mystery of growth is the message. God gives growth, and if God is taking care of the kingdom, then the kingdom will be all right. Paul pulled a divided Corinthian church together around this idea. He said, "Neither the one who plants nor the one who waters is anything, but only God who gives the growth" (1 Cor 3:7).

The spirit of God changes people, and all our activity is the meringue on the pie. It looks good, but the substance is at another level.

II. Kingdom Growth Takes Time.

"The earth produces of itself, first the stalk, then the head, then the full grain in the head" (4:28). Note the sequence. The gradual path from seed to fruit is lined out. It doesn't happen in a day. For some plants the growth process takes years. I am impatient every May and June for fresh tomatoes to "come in." I don't like those pasteboard tomatoes offered in winter and spring. To get what I want, I have to be patient. My fretting will not hurry growth.

Henry Turlington speculated that "some among his enthusiastic listeners were eager to accomplish God's will in a hurry.... You cannot force the kingdom.... His times and seasons are beyond us" (*The Broadman Bible Commentary*, vol. 8 [Nashville: Broadman Press, 1969], 303). Yet this text is more than a plea for patience. We need to see the progression of kingdom ideas. William Barclay used illustrations from British history of moral progress (*The Gospel of Mark*, 104-105). God is at work in our time if we have eyes to see. Less than 100 years ago, Jim Crow defined social custom in the South. Women were second-class citizens 100 years ago; they could not vote. Today, both groups have opportunities their grandparents never knew. I believe these illustrations are connected to kingdom ideas. God is at work in our world. But a warning—this parable does not promise inevitable progress. It does promise the rule of God will finally prevail. The rule of God comes slowly.

We can't hurry the kingdom of God, but we can't keep it from coming either. Harvest will come. In God's good time "he goes in with his sickle, because the harvest has come" (4:29). This means all the good seeds spread by saints, apostles, missionaries, and ministers are going to mature and bring an abundant harvest. No work done for God is wasted.

Sometimes we get a preview of the great harvest that will come at God's last day. I've watched youth respond to a call to Christ's service. They turn away from a life of accumulation and offer themselves to be used by God. All the good work of parents, ministers of music, Sunday school teachers, pastors, and teachers—the seed they planted takes root. At the last day, Christ will come and the hints of the kingdom will give way to the rule of God.

III. Kingdom Size Will Surprise.

"He also said, 'With what can we compare the kingdom of God, or what parable will we use for it? It is like a mustard seed, which, when sown upon the ground, is the smallest of all the seeds on earth; yet when it is sown it grows up and becomes the greatest of all shrubs, and puts forth large branches, so that the birds of the air can make nests in its shade' " (4:30-32).

I suspect there were pragmatists among those first Christians. I can hear them mumbling, "Okay. He tells us the kingdom of God is going to survive, but we have to be patient. But will there ever be enough of us to make a difference?" The question has now shifted from "Are we going to survive?" to "Are we going to thrive?"

Jesus came preaching. He gathered a small band of followers and taught them his ways. That small band came to believe Jesus was more than a rabbi/teacher. He was the promised Messiah. The group who held this idea was so small they could have been considered insignificant. In the larger social order of Rome, they were as "mustard seed," too small to matter.

But small beginnings do not always lead to small endings. The mustard seed is very small, but the mustard plant is not. William Barclay clarified, "In Palestine this mustard seed did grow into something very like a tree" (*The Gospel of Mark*, 107). Birds made their nests in the large shrub (often called a tree) that came of mustard seed.

We interpret this parable from the vantage point of 2,000 years. Time has passed. Recently, the Pope visited Canada, Guatemala, and Mexico. The crowds that came to see him were more than a million. Billy Graham led an evangelistic campaign in Cincinnati earlier this year. Thousands came. These are the headlines. Every day of the year, in quiet places, little groups gather for prayer and Bible study. Only God knows how many are in these groups.

What is the point of this recital of Christian numbers? Look what became of the 120 in Acts 1:15. The church Jesus founded has become a major world religion. (Note how I equate the kingdom of God and the church universal; the two are not the same. They are close.) We are a very large company. If only those first harassed, persecuted Christians could see what has become of the church! They would be astounded. The seed has grown. Birds have come from everywhere. The nests are large.

A caution: Size can be vulgar. Size can become more than a description of our company. Size can become the first measure of us—"If we are big we are important and blessed of God. If we are small we must not matter and God has not blessed us." Worship of the "size god" can lead to idolatry. Jesus promised, "For where two or three are gathered in my name, I am there among them" (Mt 18:20). To be large in number is not the end-all in our religion.

Conclusion

The parables answered three questions the early Christians asked as they suffered and died for the church:

(1) Are kingdom of God ideas going to survive? Will the church make it? Yes. God is in charge of the survival of the church.

(2) How long will it take for us to establish the church? Growth is a process and maturity cannot be hurried.

(3) Will the church thrive? The story about the mustard seed makes the point. Wonderful things can come of a creative minority, and they have.

The early church took heart from these parables and held on. They are our heroes, and we stand on their shoulders.

The Gospel and Miracles

Mark 5:21-24, 35-43

ORIGINALLY PUBLISHED MARCH 9, 2003

Introduction

Usually when we are dealing with miracles in the Bible, we are concerned with only one miracle. So we look carefully at the feeding of the 5,000 or the raising of Lazarus. "The Gospel and Miracles" is a larger subject, and the text only opens the door to it.

Books, articles, and essays have debated the possibility of miracles. S. V. McCasland said, "The primary question, and in a sense the only real question, in religion, is God. If one believes in God, that God creates the universe, sustains it, and controls it, most of the difficulties of miracle have thereby been dealt with" (*The Interpreter's Dictionary of the Bible*, K–Q [New York: Abingdon Press, 1962], 394-95). Since I believe in God, I open the door to the possibility of miracle. God created "natural law." Most church people believe in God and recognize the way God usually orders daily life. But our recognition of natural law does not mean natural law binds God. So, don't make "natural law" the end-all, the bottom line. This text tells of two wonderful miracles. I believe they were miracles in the truest sense. The woman was healed of a hemorrhage that doctors could not cure. The child was really dead, and Jesus really made the girl alive. What does this text say to us?

I. Desperation and Reputation Brought Them Together.

Neither Jairus nor the bleeding woman wanted to come to Jesus. Both would have preferred some other way to deal with their problems. They went to Jesus because they were desperate and knew he could help.

(1) Desperation. "Then one of the leaders of the synagogue named Jairus came and, when he saw him, fell at his feet and begged him repeatedly, 'My little daughter is at the point of death' " (Mk 5:22-23a). "Leaders of the synagogue" were not beating a path to Jesus. Mark tells of their suspicion for Jesus (see 2:6, 16, 24; 3:1-6). It was not good for a man in Jairus's position to be seen in the company of Jesus. But a sick daughter put orthodoxy on the second shelf. The first thing he needed to do was to find help for his child.

The woman was in the same shape. "Now there was a woman who had been suffering from hemorrhages for twelve years. She had endured much under many physicians, and had spent all that she had; and she was no better, but rather grew worse" (5:25-26). There is no way we can understand what she risked by coming to Jesus. She dared not openly deal with the problem; she tried to sneak a miracle from Jesus. Financially broke from her many attempts to be healed, trapped in social custom that made her perpetually "unclean" (see Lev 15:25-27), she, like Jairus, was desperate.

(2) Reputation. There is biographical sequence in Mark. He has already told of Jesus' healing the sick, stilling the storm, and casting out demons. The word of Jesus' miracles was getting around. Henry Turlington said, "Here Jesus' deeds were well known, and the hope of help drew two distraught persons to call upon him" (*The Broadman Bible Commentary*, vol. 8 [Nashville: Broadman Press, 1969], 310). We're not so different from the two hurting people in our text. The reputation of a good healer still draws desperate people.

Would these two people have been open to Jesus had they not been desperate? I don't know, but I doubt it. Hard times often drive us to places we would never have gone, and strangely, hard times can open us to God. Whatever Jairus and the sick woman thought of Jesus before, they saw him in a new light after healing.

II. Need and Faith Were All They Had.

We are saved by grace, not works, but our faith commends us to God. This part of the session is about Jairus and the sick woman. Both had qualities within them that made Jesus peculiarly open to them.

(1) Need. When Jesus called Levi (Matthew) into his service, Levi had a party. He invited all his "sinner" friends (Mk 2:15). Scribes and Pharisees saw who was at the party and criticized Jesus. Jesus answered the criticism: "Those who are well have no need of a physician, but those who are sick; I have come to call not the righteous but sinners" (Mk 2:17b). Need is a necessary piece in the text.

Jairus and the sick woman were in great need. We serve a compassionate Savior. When we hurt, God feels it. Jesus is our best picture of the nature of God, and the Gospels describe a caring Son of God. "Moved with compassion" and similar phrases appear frequently (see Mt 20:34; Lk 7:13a). Jesus responded to these two people because they were needy; when we give the same response to human need, we are acting like Jesus.

(2) Faith. I suspect Jairus went to Jesus when doctors said there was no hope. He threw himself at Jesus and with a faith born of desperation said, "My little daughter is at the point of death. Come and lay your hands on her, so that she may be made well, and live" (5:23b). The text tells us the man believed that Jesus could make his daughter well. And the same faith was in the woman who "came up behind him in the crowd and touched his cloak, for she said, 'If I but touch his clothes, I will be made well' " (5:27b-28). Luccock said of the woman, "There was a measure of what we would today call superstition in it, a suggestion of belief in the magic power of everything connected with Jesus. But it was enough to impel her to action, to the outreach of hope and faith" (*The Interpreter's Bible*, vol. 7 [New York: Abingdon Press, 1951], 721). Jesus works best in a faith environment. When he went to Nazareth, "he could do no deed of power there, except that he laid his hands on a few sick people and cured them. And he was amazed at their unbelief" (Mk 6:5-6). We don't control God or grace, but our faith looses the power of God to our good. And when faith is in short supply, the very power of God seems to shrink. Maybe this is why the apostles said to Jesus, "Increase our faith!" (Lk 17:5a). Jairus and the sick woman could not command a miracle, but their faith opened the door.

III. Miracle Forces a Question.

The four Gospels record thirty-two miracles. Our text is from Mark 5. By the time a reader gets to our text, Mark has cited nine miracles. Jesus:

• healed a man with "an unclean spirit," 1:21-28. Those who watched "were all amazed, and they kept on asking one another, 'What is this? …He commands even the unclean spirits and they obey him' " (1:27-28). Note the question.
• healed Simon's mother-in-law, 1:29-31.
• cured "many…sick…and cast out many demons," 1:32-35.
• healed a leper, 1:40-45.

- healed a paralyzed man, 2:3-13. And people "were all amazed and glorified God, saying, 'We have never seen anything like this.' " They had to wonder how Jesus did what he did. Miracles raise questions.
- healed a man with a withered hand, 3:1-6.
- "cured many, so that all who had diseases pressed upon him to touch him," 3:9-11. This tells us there were more miracles than are recorded, and the sick came to him from all over. Who is this healer?
- stilled the storm, 4:35-41. The disciples asked, "Who then is this, that even the wind and the sea obey him?" (4:41b). Again, a question.
- healed the pitiful demoniac in "the country of the Gerasenes," 5:1-20. "Everyone was amazed" (4:20b).

And then we come to our text. I've listed nine occasions when Mark tells of miracles, and I only counted those before our text. Why does Mark emphasize miracles? What is he trying to tell us? Mark's Gospel revolves around the identity of Jesus. Miracles carry powerful suggestions. They suggest an answer to the real question in Mark—who is Jesus? Pheme Perkins said, "They [miracles] served as demonstrations that God's divine power was in Jesus, the Son of God. The miracle itself provokes the question of Jesus' identity and awe over the power he exercises" (*The New Interpreter's Bible* [Nashville: Abingdon Press, 1995], 590).

Mark tells us his intention up front. In his opening sentence he tells us his message: "The beginning of the good news of Jesus Christ, the Son of God" (1:1). Mark is leading us first to identify Jesus as Son of God and then to confess faith in him.

The identity of Jesus was public discussion. Herod thought Jesus was John the Baptizer resurrected from the dead (6:14-16). Jesus asked the disciples point blank, "Who do you say that I am? Peter answered him, 'You are the Messiah' " (8:29). I believe the first eight chapters of Mark were gathered evidence in answer to the question "Who is Jesus?" The miracles were one of the ways Mark identified Jesus as Son of God.

Ancient Christians called the Gospel writers "evangelists." I used to have a more constricted view of an evangelist. He was the fellow who preached the annual revival at my home church. But the early church took a larger view. They correctly saw what I did not. Mark set out to identify Jesus. Only Jesus could accomplish the wonderful, amazing things we call miracles. Jesus' miracles forced those who witnessed them to answer the questions that flowed from them. How does he do this? Who is he? And the answer moved toward

Messiah, and that is the gospel. Miracles suggest the tight connection between Jesus and God.

Nearly 2,000 years have passed since Jesus performed those wonderful, amazing miracles. Mark's record of them appealed to a first-century audience and gained a hearing for the gospel. We are children of an age that looks at miracles with a built-in skepticism. For us, miracles raise questions. What are we to do? Do we hurry by the miracles in the Gospels, try to hide them? Do we try to "explain" them away? Shall we twist the text until some "logical" explanation can be made of them? None of the above.

Augustine said Christianity triumphed over the pagan religions of the ancient world because Christians out-lived, out-thought and out-died their rivals. Modern paganism is on the offensive. C. S. Lewis defended our faith in Oxford fifty years ago. Oxford's questions about the supernatural have come to my town, your town. If the Christian religion is going to contend for the minds of our brightest, we are going to have to do a kind of work most of us have left to others. This "comment" has only opened a door to a subject we need to explore in depth. "The Gospel and Miracles" needs a larger, longer study.

The Gospel and Proclamation

Mark 6:30-44

ORIGINALLY PUBLISHED MARCH 16, 2003

Introduction

Of all Jesus' miracles, only the feeding of the 5,000 is found in all four Gospels. It made a powerful impression. We usually emphasize the "five loaves and two fishes" and the "twelve baskets" left over. These are worthwhile themes and need to be aired, but this miracle contains more than I have preached. Jesus did not do all the preaching. Early in his ministry he began to initiate his disciples. "He called the twelve and began to send them out two by two" (Mk 6:6b-7).

Not much is made of the preaching/healing ministries of the apostles. We may be missing a piece in the puzzle. Pentecost was not the first time Peter preached; he had been on mission several times. Our text begins when a mission assignment has ended. "The apostles gathered around Jesus, and told him all that they had done and taught" (6:30). They had been trying their wings. It was all at once exciting and exhausting. Jesus saw their condition and planned some "down time." It was a good plan, but it was not to be.

I see four strong ideas in this text. The first is popularity. There would not have been 5,000 people to feed had Jesus not been popular. Then three strong teaching ideas follow. A full session could be built around each. Be careful; too many good ideas make for confusion.

I. Popularity, 6:31-33.

The disciples came back from their preaching/healing mission with what my wife calls "people fatigue." Jesus recognized their condition and planned a little trip away from the crowd. They would go across the lake to find a "deserted place all by yourselves and rest a while" (6:31).

The word that comes nearest describing the first year of the ministry of Jesus is popularity. Mark tells of a persistent crowd.

- "Many were coming and going, and they had no leisure even to eat," 6:31b.
- "Many saw them going and recognized them," 6:33a.
- "As they went ashore, he saw a great crowd," 6:34a.

Jesus and the disciples had become like today's music or movie stars. They had no time alone. The crowd was beyond welcome; they had become invasive. Jesus taught with stories people could understand; that made him popular. Jesus healed people from terrible diseases, so sick people flocked to him.

Is popularity good or bad? Actually, popularity is morally neutral. It can be good or bad, depending on what you do with it.

- If I use my popularity to enlarge myself, if I enrich myself by way of popularity, then popularity is no more than an ego trip to the bank. In this case, popularity is bad and misused.
- If I use my popularity to good cause, I can harness my influence to service. Former President Jimmy Carter is an illustration of my point. He used his popularity to build the Carter Center, which does enormous good. In his case popularity is very good.

Jesus never feasted on his popularity; he used it to higher purpose. Nor did he make decisions on the basis of "What will this decision do to my popularity?" His popularity gave him a crowd; then he taught them, fed them, healed them, loved them. That's popularity used for God's service.

II. Compassion, 6:34.

"As he went ashore, he saw a great crowd; and he had compassion for them, because they were like sheep without a shepherd; and he began to teach them many things" (6:34). Put yourself in the place of Jesus. Try to remember how tired you were after pulling together a church event. You weren't angry with anyone; you just needed some time to be alone.

Then just when it seemed that you were going to get some rest and recreation, up popped more demanding people. The unending demands of a crowd drain every bit of strength, energy, and talent.

Jesus was different from and better than I am. When he was dead tired, overworked, and in need of rest, he looked at another crowd of hurting people and "had compassion for them." I've said the crowd was demanding. They were, but I also give them some credit. They instinctively knew Jesus had the answers they were seeking. Life is hard for most people.
They live from paycheck to paycheck, struggling to make ends meet. Barclay put it well: "Life can be so bewildering. We can stand at some crossroads of life and not know what way to take" (*The Gospel of Mark* [Philadelphia: Westminster Press, 1956], 157).

Our text prompted Halford Luccock to ask, "Which comes most naturally to us, irritation or compassion?" (*The Interpreter's Bible*, vol. 7 [New York: Abingdon Press, 1951], 740). We are not made of the same stuff Jesus was, but we are supposed to be edging in his direction. A Christian is one who takes on the nature of Jesus; so I ought to be changing from a self-centered, self-absorbed person into a service person. This change is conversion, and it usually takes place over an extended period of time. When I am fully Christian I will give "Jesus responses" to life situations. Compassion is simply feeling with and caring about the needs of another. When we show compassion we crawl out of ourselves and into the shoes of a hurting person. Jesus had a lot of compassion.

III. Responsibility, 6:35-37.

Jesus began to teach the crowd. Time passed quickly because he held them spellbound, and then it was late in the afternoon. Remember the setting: an uninvited crowd who had pushed their way into a day that was supposed to be given to rest and retreat. I have some sympathy for the disciples who said, "This is a deserted place, and the hour is now very late; send them away so that they may go into the surrounding country and villages and buy something for themselves to eat" (6:35b-36). With some justification the disciples were saying, "They are not our responsibility."

What the disciples were saying made sense, and what they said is replayed in our time again and again.

- The city council discusses immigrants who have moved into town. They were not invited; they just "showed up." These people have needs, lots of them. The disciples are there to say, "they are not our responsibility."
- Congress is discussing care for children. The disciples are there; one says, "they are not our responsibility."
- The finance committee is at work at church. The sticking point is the missions budget. Do we help the poor yet more? One of the disciples speaks up. He says, "We do enough already; they are not our responsibility."

But the disciples did not get the last word. In response to their "send them away," Jesus said, "You give them something to eat" (6:35-37a). The disciples answered, "Are we to go and buy two hundred denarii worth of bread, and give it to them to eat?" (6:37b). An average worker earned one denarius a day; the disciples estimated it would take 200 denarii to buy enough to feed the crowd (see Turlington, *The Broadman Bible Commentary*, vol. 8 [Nashville: Broadman Press, 1969], 319). They didn't have that kind of money, and in a "deserted place" they could not have found that much food to buy. What Jesus said made no sense.

If you think about it, the tasks assigned the church make no sense. We are supposed to "Go therefore and make disciples of all nations" (Mt 28:19a). The church does not have that kind of money. We are supposed to respond in love and compassion to all in need. We don't have that kind of energy or resources. It's not just compassion that is in short supply; we don't have enough hard cash to do all the good that needs to be done. Compared to industry or technology or banking, church is a low-budget outfit.

This parable has no "teaching" attached. The Gospels let it stand alone. This means any "comment" I make is going beyond the text. Consider:

- There is a kind of thinking that is practical, realistic, and truthful. It is not wicked, but faith is not in the calculation. This kind of thinking is not always bad; sometimes it is necessary.
- There is another kind of thinking that mixes the practical with a little faith. A little faith can make us see things in a different light. Jesus said, "If you had faith the size of a mustard seed, you could say to this mulberry tree, 'Be uprooted and planted in the sea,' and it would obey you" (Lk 17:6a).

Often I've heard well-intentioned people say, "The church is a business," and in a sense it is. But church is a business that looks at human need with realism and a dab of faith. Jesus saw the hungry crowd through faith glasses, and that's the way we need to see them too. "You give them something to eat" is a command for the church.

IV. Resources, 6:38-44.

My pastor preached on this text in August. With a word-picture that has lingered in my mind, he said, "How many times has the devil whispered, 'It's a good cause, but you don't have enough'?" Realism trumps faith. Need goes begging. We retreat into calculation. We quit on faith and never give God a chance. We do nothing. But our text is not the church calculating; this is Jesus checking resources.

"And he said to them, 'How many loaves have you? Go and see.' When they had found out, they said, 'Five loaves and two fish'" (6:38). John's Gospel gives more detail. He tells us Andrew found some food. "There is a boy here who has five barley loaves and two fish. But what are they among so many people?" (Jn 6:9). Jesus seemed to think it was enough. "Then he ordered them to get all the people to sit down in groups on the green grass" (Mk 6:39), and then the real resources of Jesus came into play. He held the food in his hands, lifted it toward heaven, "and blessed and broke the loaves" (6:41). And like a pastor with the Lord's Supper, he passed the bread and fish to the disciples, who distributed it to the hungry people. And before their eyes a miracle! It would seem so little food would soon be gone, but that is not the way it was. Jesus must have been breaking bread and cutting fish for an hour or two. The food did not run out. There was more and more until there was enough. Everyone ate until they were filled. In fact, food was left over (see 6:43).

Most commentators see similarities in the feeding of the 5,000 and miracles in the Old Testament (see Ex 18:25). Others make much of the way this miracle previews the Lord's Supper, where Jesus blessed, broke, and gave food to his own. Still others are convinced that this miracle anticipates the great feast in heaven where Jesus will welcome and serve the saints assembled. However, what I see in this text is a miracle that is repeated in every generation. Jesus takes a little. His blessing makes it sacred and what seemed so small and insignificant becomes enough. Need is met. The message is delivered. The miracle of multiplication goes on. So in my own experience I've witnessed the multiplying power of Jesus.

People still offer Jesus their "five loaves and two fishes" lives. He doesn't toss us off, saying, "This is not enough to get the job done." Rather, he holds us high to heaven, blesses the little we are, and begins to break and distribute us to hungry people. This miracle goes on and on and on.

Healed by Touch

Mark 7:31-37

ORIGINALLY PUBLISHED SEPTEMBER 28, 1997

Introduction

Our last miracle lesson comes from Mark's Gospel. Jesus had been on a long, wandering trip. He and the disciples walked out of Galilee into Phoenicia (the region of Tyre and Sidon). This trip may have taken as long as eight months. During those eight months Jesus was able to give a compressed the-ological education to his disciples (see Barclay, *The Gospel of Mark* [Philadelphia: Westminster Press, 1956], 183-84). Jesus was sharpening the insights of the disciples, preparing them for the crucifixion and resurrection. For sure, he was helping them to identify him. He was the Messiah; the dis-ciples had to come to know this with their heads and feel it with their hearts.

As soon as the group returned to the Galilee district, they were recognized. At this point our text picks up the story. There was a "deaf man who had an impediment in his speech" (7:32a). Some friends brought the poor fellow to Jesus and "begged him to lay his hand on him" (7:32b). William Tyndale gives a most colorful description of the man: He was "deffe and stambed in his speech" (Barclay, 184). If a person can't hear, he can't know how to form words. Obviously, he will have a speech problem. Deafness and poor speech go together. This also accounts for why friends had to bring the deaf man to Jesus. If he could not hear, he could not know Jesus was in the region.

I. Consideration.

I am always amazed at the grace and good manners of Jesus. He had all the power in the world. He had the gift of performing miracles. But when he came near ordinary people, and especially when he came near hurting people, he was always kind. Consider how he treated the man in this story: "He took him aside in private, away from the crowd" (7:33a). Put yourself in the deaf man's place. He had been the butt of jokes all his life. Because he could not hear, he spoke in a way that made people not understand him. I suspect they often laughed at him. He had grown accustomed to their laughter. He could do nothing about it. He had to try to communicate, but when he tried, he came off the fool. Being around people brought embarrassment and pain.

Then into his life came a stranger. Instead of hanging him out for all to see, Jesus took the deaf man away from the gawking crowd. He found a private place. Whatever was going to happen would happen in a way and in a place that would not hurt the man who already had hurt enough.

Most of the time we are considerate. But sometimes we get so caught up in tasks that we forget people. We forget their feelings. We especially have trouble putting ourselves in the place of someone like this deaf fellow. We don't mean to be unthinking, but we are. This verse speaks a word to all who would follow Jesus: Care for the feelings of hurting people.

II. Means.

Jesus used means the deaf man could comprehend. First, he "put his fingers into his ears" (7:33b). This was the part that needed a miracle. The deaf man would understand this. Next, Jesus took some saliva from his mouth and touched the deaf man's tongue, the part that could not speak well. Ancients believed that saliva had the power to heal. Then, Jesus looked toward heaven. The deaf man would know Jesus was asking for God's aid in doing a miracle. Finally, Jesus "sighed and said to him, 'Ephphatha,' that is, 'Be opened.' " (7:34b). This sequence might communicate with a deaf person who had trouble with his speech. The effect was instant. "Immediately his ears were opened, his tongue was released, and he spoke plainly" (7:35).

Too often I want the religious experience of all people to be like mine. I think some folks are too emotional about their religion. It seems to me some people are too rational, and others are too charismatic for me. But who am I to use my bias to set the standard for the religious experiences of others? God will work a miracle in the lives of people any way God chooses. And I am the one who needs to adjust. I suspect Jesus still deals with people in ways they can understand. This means there are several ways. And I must open my mind to let Jesus work in a way that makes sense to the one on whom a miracle is being wrought.

III. Affirmations.

In Mark, Jesus often tells people not to tell anyone what he has done for them. That is the case here. "Jesus ordered them to tell no one" (7:36a). But when you think about it, that would be hard to do. The man has been unable to speak plainly; now he can. If he doesn't speak, he doesn't use his new gift. The miracle is put to no effect. If he does speak, he is disobedient. The fellow opts to speak. "But the more he ordered them, the more zealously they proclaimed it" (7:36b). Every time the man opened his mouth, and no matter what he said, he bore witness to the healing power of Jesus.

The healing had an effect. People "were astounded beyond measure, saying, 'He has done everything well; he even makes the deaf to hear and the mute to speak' " (7:37). Isn't this what Jesus came to do? Where there was sickness, he brought health. Where there was lostness, he brought salvation. It reminds us of the line used at the Creation. At the end of the third day, "God saw that it was good" (Gen 1:12). And then at the end of the sixth day of Creation, "God saw everything that he had made, and indeed, it was very good. And there was evening and morning, the sixth day" (Gen 1:31). Actually, this is theology written on a large scale. Eden's damage is being undone. Jesus is making wrongs right. One by one, piece by piece, the lost are being found, the sick are being made well, the confused are sorting things out.

IV. Clues.

The people who witnessed this miracle knew their Old Testament. They knew that the long-sought Messiah was supposed to be able to do miracles. Isaiah had told them, "Then the eyes of the blind shall be opened, and the ears of the deaf unstopped; then the lame shall leap like a deer, and the tongue of the speechless sing for joy" (Isa 35:5-6).

What had Jesus done? He had done the things promised of the One who would be the Messiah. Slowly, they began to piece it together. They broke free from tradition and the culture that bound them. They broke free to see a new revelation in Jesus.

Mark's Gospel has a firm chronology. By the end of chapter 8, Jesus was telling the disciples of his coming crucifixion and testing them about his identity. Jesus was asking, "Who do people say that I am?...But who do you say that I am?" (8:27b, 29a). To get the right answer to the questions, the disciples had to get clues from miracles such as the one in our text today. The miracles suggested who Jesus was. They carried a heavy theology, but they carried it in subtle fashion. Miracles did not declare Jesus to be the Messiah; they merely suggested it.

Clues, hints, suggestions: These are the ways Jesus identified himself upon his own. It is his way even now. A lot of people want Jesus to come at them with point-blank statements. They want special revelations. Rarely does God work that way. Nearly always he comes in forms that surprise us. Who would have supposed the Messiah would come to Bethlehem as a baby? Who would have imagined the message to the Gentiles would come through one who had once persecuted the church? Who would have imagined the gospel preached in these days would come through some of the unlikely people who are "vehicles of grace"?

Faith is taking a chance on something you "believe" to be so but is beyond proof. God's clue has to be matched by our faith in order for the message and the Messiah to come clear. In Christ, God was not hiding from us. Actually, God was revealing God's self in clearest form.

Helping God Help You

Mark 14:1-11

ORIGINALLY PUBLISHED OCTOBER 24, 1999

Introduction

I come from a middle-class background. I think I am fortunate because I had to learn to work. I had to learn frugality because my family didn't have enough to waste. We had to live by some disciplines; without discipline, we would not have made it.

Once in a while I find a story in the Bible that clashes with my middle-class values. In fact, my middle-class values and the gospel are often a train wreck. If I am to understand the gospel, I am going to have to change, rethink.

For instance, when I was young I often criticized extravagant expressions of Christian devotion. Whenever an expensive sanctuary was built, I would lament, "This ointment could have been sold for more than three hundred denarii, and the money given to the poor" (Mk 14:5 NRSV). Similarly, when I first viewed the great cathedrals of the Old World, I remarked, "This ointment could have been sold, and just think of all the missionaries we might have sent to the third world."

The disciples would have understood my introduction. Growing up in Galilee under Roman rule must have been hard. In fact, there was no way but to work hard and save every penny. As for extravagance? Well, extravagance was always wrong. It was considered the way of the idle rich. All gifts had to be prudent, for life itself had to be prudent.

And then the woman broke the alabaster jar of pure nard; it was one year's wages for a middle-class worker. It was unthinkable! Though they lived in a different culture, the disciples had many of the same values we do. And right before their eyes a gift was made in the most extravagant way. Something precious was poured out, spent, forever used—by all human standards, wasted. But Jesus praised the woman! Our lesson really hinges on a collision of values. The way Jesus saw what the woman did and the way I see it need to come closer together. And I suspect I am not alone in needing to move closer to Jesus' perception on this text.

I. She Broke the Jar, 14:3.

Every Gospel recounts this story; it made a powerful impression on the apostles. Jesus was nearing the cross. He was making his way to Jerusalem, and Bethany was on the way. Death hovered like a dark cloud over Jesus, but he was not surprised by his circumstances.

But there were social moments. Simon the leper entertained Jesus in his home. Mary, Martha, and Lazarus lived in Bethany and were at the dinner as well. John identifies Mary as the one who broke the alabaster jar (see Jn 12:2). It is hard for us to recreate what Mary did. Her act was extravagant beyond anything words can describe.

Nard was extracted from a plant native to India and stored in a stone jar manufactured at Alabastron, Egypt. So popular was the type of jar made at Alabastron that the stone has come to be known simply as alabaster. This jar would have had a long neck. Mary brought the jar, broke the neck, and completely emptied the nard on the head and feet of Jesus. It was an act of extreme extravagance, and the extravagance certainly did not go unnoticed.

I've told you what happened, but more important than the act itself was the selfless giving of the woman. She did not calculate, "Well, that ought to be enough." She went beyond calculation to abandonment. "This is the self-forgetfulness, the self-denial, which is a mark of the kingdom of God" (Halford E. Luccock, *The Interpreter's Bible*, vol. 7 [New York: Abingdon Press, 1951], 868).

The tragedy of our lives is that we rarely ever break through the wall of calculation. We are always thinking, measuring. But once in a lifetime someone breaks through the wall and empties a life, a bank account, a rare jewel, giving all they have. The tragedy of life for too many fine church people is that we never find the freedom of giving everything we have to Jesus. We sing about giving all to Jesus. We admire the few who do. We intend to do something extravagant for Jesus someday, but no occasion seems appropriate enough. We are saving it for a better, later opportunity. Life slips by while we measure ourselves out with a medicine dropper, worried that we should spend a drop more than "the Law" requires. What a pity. We never break the jar.

II. This Ointment Might Have Been Sold…and Given to the Poor, 14:5.

I can almost hear the disciples gasp, "Did you see what she poured on Jesus?" It took everyone by surprise, and the reasonable response should have been "What generosity!" That was not forthcoming.

Instead, the disciples questioned: "Why was the ointment wasted in this way? For this ointment could have been sold for more than three hundred denarii, and the money given to the poor" (14:4b-5). Jesus responded, "Let her alone; why do you trouble her? She has performed a good service for me. For you always have the poor with you, and you can show kindness to them whenever you wish…" (14:6-7). This text needs some interpretation, for it is often misinterpreted.

Is this justification for insensitivity to the poor? Think of the larger ministry of Jesus. It was his pattern to take care of the poor. He fed, healed, and spent his ministry reaching out to people in need.

So if this is the way of Jesus, then what was wrong with the disciples' question? Timing. This was no time for ordinary charity. The disciples had no sense of the moment. Jesus had been telling them for weeks (ever since Caesarea Philippi) that he was soon to die. And the disciples missed it. There are daily charities and then there are a few times in life when more is required. Knowing when, sensing the moment, is the sign of the soul's being in touch with God. In those few holy moments, it is appropriate to set aside the care of the poor and do the extravagant thing. So do we care for the poor? Yes. Every day we ought to care for the poor. But there are moments when something really extravagant is in order.

III. She Has Performed a Good Service for Me, 14:6b.

The RSV translates this phrase, "She has done a beautiful thing to me," an interpretation that I think comes nearest to what Jesus actually said. To do a "good thing," the Greek uses "agothos," meaning "good," but the word used here is "kalos," which means "a thing which is not only good but lovely" (William Barclay, *The Gospel of Mark* [Philadelphia: Westminster Press, 1956], 342). I doubt the Lord will find most of us wanting in doing good, but we may be lacking for doing the "lovely" thing. I usually resort to the practical.

There are times in life when the only thing to do is let go. I recall when I first met Dot Hair. She was the loveliest girl I had ever seen. I wanted her to think well of me. But alas, I was just an average seminarian and penniless. But somehow I managed to muster up the courage to ask her to dinner. To my delight, she said yes. I found the nicest place in town. It was expensive. I called ahead and made reservations. In fact, I even went by the place, studied the menu, and placed our orders in advance. When we walked in, the head-waiter called me by name. The meal was elegant. I had broken my jar, gotten my foot in the door with the girl of my dreams.

Is the extravagance of that first dinner the way Dot and I have lived the past forty-five years? Not at all. But that was the extravagance of first love. Am I glad I did it? Why, I'd do it again in a New York minute. I missed noon meals for two weeks to pay for that evening, but I still reap dividends on that investment. Once in my life I gave myself away. I was totally extravagant. I did a beautiful thing. Sometime in my life I must do a beautiful thing for Jesus.

IV. She Has Done What She Could, 14:8a.

I suspect some of you are pondering what the woman did for Jesus. When I said "sometime do a beautiful thing for Jesus," you might have begun to speculate about how grand it would be to do a magnificent, awesome thing. All of us have done this. I fantasize, "If I had a million dollars, I'd do this or that good thing." It is easier to fantasize about something we can't do than to think seriously of what we can do.

Mary did not have much to give Jesus. The glory of what Mary did is that she gave the gift she had. She did what she could.

The mind is an amazing thing. After we have fantasized about what we would do if we had this or that, we somehow factor the thought in a way that makes us passive. We reason with ourselves, "Since I don't have a million dollars, I can't make an extravagant gift. And since I had a noble thought, I am sure God will give me credit for generosity simply because I fantasized about offering a generous gift I don't have."

The kingdom of God runs by different standards. Jesus has put extravagance on a sliding scale. When he watched what people put into the treasury, he commended the woman who put in the least gift. Jesus said the poor widow's gift was actually the largest of all (see Mk 12:41-44). I refer to what we call "the widow's mite." For the widow, the gift was extravagant. Mary and the poor widow put the extravagant gift within reach of us all.

V. You Will Not Always Have Me, 14:7b.

We don't have Mary's motivation. Jesus is not about to die. But don't dismiss this word too quickly. Time is not short for Jesus, we are the ones who run out of time. If I could modify "You will not always have me," I would say instead, "We will not always have the chance to do an extravagant thing for Jesus."

Time is moving swiftly. Many of us are old. Anything we do for Jesus, we have to do quickly. We've lived prudently, measured our gifts, calculated. If there is going to be one shining moment when we escape calculation to act out of extravagant love, the time will have to be soon.

But most of us are not near the end of life. Hopefully, we have many years ahead of us. What's the hurry?

I have a question for you. Should you suppress the extravagant impulse? The clue to greatness in the Christian life lies near. When we have a strong impulse to do something grand and beautiful for Jesus and his Church, we are at our best. And we need to act on that impulse. It most surely came from the Spirit. If we are simply impulsive by nature and have such impulses everyday, then I will be the first to restrain an impulsive lifestyle. But that is not the sin of most of us.

Once Jesus was passing down the road. Some good men had an inclination to follow him and become disciples. But upon more thoughtful consideration, one said, "Lord, first let me go and bury my father" (Lk 9:59b). And another said, "I will follow you, Lord; but let me first say farewell to those at my home" (Lk 9:61). Those men never became disciples. They had an extravagant impulse, postponed it, and the moment was lost. They never felt that way again. Even more unfortunate, Jesus never passed that way again. In fact, we never even hear of them again.

There's a little bit of Mary locked down inside the souls of us all. There's a precious treasure hidden away in the closet of our lives, too. Find the gift. Do the lovely, beautiful thing! When Mary made the gift, he said, "Truly I tell you, wherever the good news is proclaimed in the whole world, what she has done will be told in remembrance of her" (14:9). Therefore, this lesson is "in remembrance of her." And the prophecy of Jesus is true.

Have You Denied Yourself?

Mark 8:27–9:1

ORIGINALLY PUBLISHED FEBRUARY 27, 1994

Introduction

Today's question comes at both a critical time and place in the ministry of Jesus.

(1) The time was late. Jesus took the disciples on one last retreat/journey just before he "turned his face toward Jerusalem." The teachings of this last intense session with the disciples are among the most difficult of all Jesus pressed upon them. Jesus did not ask mature thinking and severe discipleship early in his ministry. By the end he was asking the disciples to be willing to live, suffer and die as he did.

(2) The place was remote. On a trip to the Holy Land some fifteen lyears ago our guide took us "into the district of Caesarea Philippi" (Mt 16:13a NRSV). Until this day that district is lonesome, far removed from city life. If you were looking for a retreat setting, Caesarea Philippi is still an option. In that quiet place, removed from the hurried push and shove of the life of a miracle worker, Jesus set out to fine tune the minds of his disciples. And remember, it was just before betrayal, trial and crucifixion. I suspect the disciples often reflected on the sanity and the beauty of that last walk with Jesus. After the resurrection the teachings of Caesarea Philippi would make more sense.

Now I am going to offer you an outline for organizing this text. It is not the only way to divide and emphasize this material. It is one way. If it proves helpful, I will be pleased. Use the parts that seem to you to be the best interpretation of the text.

I. Recognizing Jesus, 8:27-30.

The pathway led north. The pace would test them, for the journey is upward. Caesarea Philippi was at the foot of Mount Hermon and was near the source of the Jordan River. This was high country. I suspect only the apostle band was with Jesus at the time he asked the question that mattered.

Notice the teaching technique. "Who do people say that I am?" (Mk 8:27b NRSV). "But who do you say that I am?" (Mk 8:29 NRSV). The first question did not press them. They simply reported what people were saying about Jesus the miracle worker. Then Jesus bore into the minds of the twelve and asked, "But who do you say that I am?"

Peter was the spokesman. He seems to have answered quickly and correctly. "You are the Messiah" (Mk 8:29b NRSV). And as I peck these words from my old typewriter they seem so tame. It is old news. All church people know the right answer to the question. But the power in the text is ours only if we can turn back the clock and recreate the awesomeness of what Peter said.

I am going to speculate. I think the disciples had talked among themselves about who Jesus was before this question was asked. They had to. At some point in time reasonable people had to try to understand who this person is who commands the winds and the waves, who orders demons out of the possessed, who makes lame people to walk and blind people to see. There had been too much that was beyond rational explanation. Of course with the passing of time Jesus has become a friend, but he was different and more. He had to be explained. I don't think this question was unanticipated. If I am right then that would help to explain why Peter gave the right answer too, quickly.

Entry-level Christianity begins with getting the right answer to this question. Who is Jesus? That is the beginning point. If Jesus is just another of the prophets, then that is good but not so unusual. From time to time God had crowded into time and space and spoken through the prophets. But Jesus was more than another prophet. Jesus was and remains revelation lifted to highest power. Christians are the people who see God through the words and ways of Jesus.

So, one part of becoming a Christian is "recognizing Jesus." There is a heavy line in the Appalachian Christmas carol, "Sweet Little Jesus Boy." The author was trying to explain why all of us have treated Jesus badly. And the explanation line runs like this, "We didn't know who you was." Everything starts with getting straight the first question, "But who do you say that I am?" And the evangelist is right. Everyone has to answer that question. Messiah is not a word we use readily. Technical definitions are unnecessary;

practical definitions are. It means God's special revelation and our special hope. The one who is Messiah is both.

II. Understanding Jesus, 8:31-33.

"Then he began to teach them that the Son of Man must undergo great suffering, and be rejected by the elders...and be killed, and after three days rise again" (Mk 8:31 NRSV). Jewish expectation had taken over the idea of Messiah. In the popular mind the Messiah would be successor to King David. And King David was associated with the glory era of Jewish history. The coming of Messiah would usher in a time of Jewish glory. There would be military power and prosperity. The coming of Messiah would be a good time, a grand time, a glorious time. The words of Jesus did not fit the expectation. He moved from Peter's answer ("You are the Messiah") to teaching about suffering, rejection and death. The two ideas did not fit comfortably, and they still don't.

The appeal made to most of us at the time we "became Christians" is that if we will repent of our sins and follow Jesus our lives will get better. We will live a full and abundant life and when we die will go to heaven.

Or, the appeal is put another way: Are you tired of guilt and sin? Are you tired of being down on yourself and feeling like you are trash? Do you want to feel better about yourself and get out from under the heavy loads of guilt and shame and sin? Then come to Jesus.

The trouble with what I am saying is that there is a germ of truth in all the popular expectation. Jesus does make our lives better. Jesus does take away our sin and our shame and our guilt. And Jesus does mark the way to a better life. But that is only part of the story.

Listen to Paul as he works through his own expectations in following Jesus, "I want to know Christ and the power of his resurrection and the sharing of his sufferings by becoming like him in his death, if somehow I may attain the resurrection of the dead" (Phil. 3:19 NRSV). The parallels to Mark 8:31 are amazing. Jesus spoke of suffering, rejection and death that would come before resurrection. Paul repeated the same sequence. He expected the same sequence. He did not think that Jesus would suffer and be rejected and die, but he would not. Rather, he saw that the path to glory led along the same route for us that it did for him. Jesus really did mark the way.

Too many people have "come to Jesus" wanting all the good and somehow being blind to all the price. I'm not sure there is a real Christianity that can give us all the good parts of being a Christian without the suffering, rejection and death. Jesus "paid it all," but Jesus did not intend to spare us the reasonable costs of discipleship.

At this point I imagine some will wonder if it really costs so much to be a disciple. It has not been their experience. So, why should it be pattern? But stark honesty in a world of ethical relativity will get you suffering, rejection and career death. Compassion in an uncaring world will get expensive. Fairness in a very unfair society will only bring grief. A pagan, hostile society still treats Jesus people just like that society treated Jesus a long, long time ago. And nowhere is this rule more true than in the world of organized religion.

III. Following Jesus, 8:34-9:1.

Then Jesus gave an invitation. "If any want to become my followers, let them deny themselves and take up their cross and follow me" (Mk 8:34b NRSV). It is from this text that the lesson gets its title.

We live in an indulgent time. Even good Christians are pampered when compared to the more severe times of our grandparents. So, the idea of self-denial is outside our experience. All of us see people who have little, but the reason they have little is because they have been unable either to inherit or acquire the good things. Even the people who have little are not in a state of self-denial. If they could have the good life they would take it in a "New York minute." Self-denial is choosing to walk away from the luxuries and the comforts of this life.

A few years ago my wife and I came upon the biography of St. Francis. In that story we found real self-denial. He was born to wealth; his father was a prosperous cloth merchant. His youth was filled with excess and self-indulgence. But as a young man he came to a true turning point, a conversion. He determined to try to live the life Jesus asked of us all. He gave away his wealth. He became a friend of the powerless, the sick, the imprisoned. He cast himself on the provision of God; each day he begged what he ate. Francis who as a young man had many changes of clothing, came as an older man to have but one suit of clothes. A more accommodating religion tolerated him, humored him. But the people who watched saw in St. Francis some one who was in the true pattern of Jesus. So, young men and women wanted to follow him in his self-denial. A band of followers grew up around him who are now called Franciscans, or the people who imitate the life style and thought of St. Francis. St. Francis was into self-denial.

There are modern illustrations of self-denial. Some of the brightest and best of my generation gave up certain prosperity for a life of missionary service. They have not done without; they walked out on the good life for a more Jesus way. I am convinced the reason Jesus is followed but carelessly in our time is the reluctance of modern Christianity to put before people self-denial.

In these days the religion of self-fulfillment is popular. God means for us to have riches...at least that is what some TV preachers will tell you. That is straight in the face of today's text, and it is misrepresentation of the Jesus way. It is bad religion.

Then Jesus goes on to say, "For those who want to save their life will lose it, and those who lose their life for my sake, and for the sake of the gospel, will save it" (Mk 8:35 NRSV). Note that just a Spartan self-denial can be pagan. It is self-denial "for the sake of the gospel" that will commend us to God. And such self-denial will put us in sync with eternal things. There is a way that is passing, ephemeral and eternally of no consequence. Gathering things and the notice of this world is transient. But when we enter into the work of Jesus, we enter into a different sphere. To invest the self in eternal things "will save" their lives into another world and into God's heaven. This is the word of Jesus.

Too much of me is tied up in stuff that will pass away. Too much time, too much wealth, too much worry is wrapped up in this world. I am like most people. Probably you are more like me than you are like St. Francis or any modern saint. But following Jesus is heavier stuff than most of us have sampled much less modeled. Following Jesus is getting into self-denial.

Are You First or Last?

Mark 9:30-50

ORIGINALLY PUBLISHED MARCH 6, 1994

Introduction

I think this question gets at a level of discipleship beyond the norm. It touches on radical, serious, life-ordering religion.

Jesus is still fine-tuning and reinforcing and saying again what he wants the disciples to know. The road to Jerusalem is before him. The cross is near. Time is running out. There is an urgency about Jesus not found in the earlier parts of Mark. And the disciples are so slow. Culture has them in a vice, and Jesus is trying to redefine Messiah and service and even religion.

So, the text opens with Jesus saying "The Son of Man is to be betrayed into human hands, and they will kill him, and three days after being killed, he will rise again" (Mk 9:31 NRSV). Jesus did not want the cross to be a surprise to the twelve. Repeatedly he warned them, prepared them. But they could not hear him. I don't think the disciples were unable to learn. Quite the opposite. They were exceptionally bright and open people; later events confirm this estimate of them. But they could not hear because all their prior religious/cultural instruction had inclined them to think a certain way. The Messiah was to be a certain kind of person, and the Messiah would perform in a certain kind of way. Jesus was not in sync with all they had been conditioned to receive from "the Messiah." So, all at once they got the right answer when asked who Jesus was (see Mk 8:29b), but that the Messiah should suffer and die was beyond their comprehension.

There are parts of our minds that are just as trapped and just as encased in American culture as were the minds of the disciples. Some of these places where the culture traps me I suspect; other places I haven't a clue. Then Jesus pushed beyond anticipating the cross. He changed the subject. And now we come to the lesson. Let me offer you a way to develop the text. Take all or any part that helps.

I. Who is the Greatest? 9:33-35.

Occasionally Mark pulls back the curtain and lets a little light on the aside conversations of the disciples. As they had walked into Capernaum the disciples had gotten into an argument about "who was the greatest" (Mk 9:34 NRSV). This is interesting, for as it worked out, Peter would come to be first among equals. But apparently Peter did not come to speak for the apostles without some overt, conscious discussion by the apostles. And I want to make a guess: I think what began as rivalry progressed to a more serious level. When Jesus rose from the dead and went back to heaven and when Pentecost came upon them…when all these things happened I think the discussion about leadership and the question of who will speak for the group shifted to a much higher plane. Then it was not so much who is going to get to be "out front" but rather who will represent our cause the best? But the conversation about "who was the greatest" began in a petty argument. Jesus was aware of their rivalry and saw the argument as a chance to teach a principle.

That principle is still trying to find acceptance in the Church Christ established. The principle is simply stated: if we want to have the first place in Christ's work, we have to be willing to be the servant of everyone. Now this stands on its ear all we have heard all our lives. Rich people have servants. Servants do all the dirty work. Powerful and rich people don't have to bother themselves with the little stuff; let the servants do it. We will busy ourselves with "affairs of state." And of course, important people associate with important people.

When I was a college student the Youth Evangelism movement burst upon the world where I lived. All of a sudden the preachers were of my generation. College people were saying the gospel; I was a college person. I wanted to have a place. The Student Department of the Baptist General Convention of Texas became the place where all this activity centered. People in the student department decided who would go out to the churches. The churches asked for teams from the leadership at the Student Department. So, to be a youth evangelist one had to be commended, blessed by the people in Dallas. I recall the day I got an invitation to the instructional meeting that took place in February (I had made the first cut). I recall the nervousness

---

about assignments. Who would be sent to ten churches in the course of the summer? Who would be given but four revivals?

Browning Ware went through this process with more poise than most of us. He saw that some of us were not as gifted as others. He called us "the second string." What we were about was the strangest mix. In part we wanted to serve Christ and help young people to Christ. In another way we wanted to be first and be seen and be out front; it was very competitive. I thought of this strange paradox when I began unpacking this text. I have lived through that argument about greatness...and I am not very proud of it.

I have to assume the disciples were as self-aware as I am. I knew when I was arguing about greatness that I was into the underside of religion. All at once I was competitive and I was ashamed of myself for being competitive. And probably the disciples knew better than they were performing too. If they hadn't known better they would not have been silent when Jesus questioned them. All of us know a lot more religion than we practice. The reason we have the lesson is to get our practice up to our principle.

II. Who Is the Competition? 9:38-41.

"Teacher, we saw someone casting out demons in your name, and we tried to stop him, because he was not following us" (Mk 9:38 NRSV). Again, Mark gives us some extra insight into the energy that surrounded Jesus. There must have been layers of discipleship only slightly understood by us or recorded by the Gospels. Here is someone or a group who are going about casting out demons in the name of Jesus. And they must have had some success at what they were about.

The response of the disciples was to franchise Jesus. If there were maverick groups/individuals who were going about doing good in the name of Jesus, they had to get permission from the disciples. The disciples were going to become an approving body. If you went out in the name of Jesus, you had to get the imprimatur or permission of the disciple band. What we are into here is control. And though the second question about competition seems distant from the first about "who is first," the relation between the two is direct.

Hear the response of Jesus. "Do not stop him; for no one who doe a deed of power in my name will be able soon afterward to speak evil of me. Whoever is not against us is for us" (Mk 9:39b-40 NRSV). What bothered the disciples did not bother Jesus at all. Anyone who could do good and help people and give some semblance of the gospel, that someone was to be blessed and encouraged. So, "Whoever is not against us is for us," needs to become the rule of fellowship.

III. Who Is the Child? 9:36-37, 42-48.

I have purposely combined the two places in the text that refer to the child (vv. 36-37, 42-47). And again, though the connection between "Who is Greatest?" and "Who is the Child?" may seem distant, upon closer examination, the relationship is immediate. When Jesus was dealing with "Who is the Greatest?" he reached for the child (see v. 36).

Servanthood and children go hand in hand. The people who care for the children in our society are not the "power people." It is not an accident people want to farm out the care of the child. It is not by chance that school teachers are underpaid and under-appreciated in America. A beginning engineer fresh out of college will likely make more money than a teacher with twenty years of good experience in city school system. So, though the time gap is two thousand years an though the culture chasm is about as wide as it can get (the difference between the ancient Middle East and modern America), the illustration still holds. If you want to make a point about service, reach for the child.

Children are powerless, helpless, vulnerable. More than any other class or group, children have been run over by the social changes that have come in modern life. When Jesus wanted to make a point about servanthood, he spoke of "Whoever welcomes one such child in my name welcomes me, and whoever welcomes me welcomes not me but the one who sent me" (Mk 9:37 NRSV). What he was saying was that the child was a symbol of service. And the care of the child was of high priority both because of the intrinsic nature/worth of the child and because of the life of service such care of the child would involve. He approved such a life of self-forgetfulness, and God approves. This is an illustration of "Whoever wants to be first must be last of all and servant of all" (Mk 9:35b NRSV). Then the part about the child moves to another thought.

"If any of you put a stumbling block before one of these little ones who believe in me, it would be better for you if a great millstone were hung around your neck and you were thrown into the sea" (Mk 9:42 NRSV). And then illustrations are offered about how "it is better for you...." The idea being that we would be better off in God's sight were we to lose a hand or a foot or an eye than that we cause one of "these little ones" to stumble or come to unbelief. I know of no more terrifying Scripture about responsibility than this text. The weight put upon the teacher of the child, upon the teacher of youth, upon the preacher at a church camp—that weight is frightening. We are to exercise our stewardship in a way that leads to larger faith and more earnest devotion. And were we to be the cause of their drifting away from God and his ways, we would put our souls at hazard. So, not only is the care of the child unappreciated by our society, in the sight of God the care of the child is the heaviest responsibility.

Conclusion

The text is wrapped up in two verses at the very end (Mk 9:49 50). Jesus tells us to hold fast to two ideals:

(1) "Salt is good, but if salt has lost its saltiness, how can you season it?" (Mk 9:50a NRSV). This is exactly the same idea used in the Sermon on the Mount (Mt 5:13). We are to be different people. We are to season this bland or tasteless world with a flavor that makes a difference. If truly we are the people who serve and measure greatness by service, then we will be salt. In my generation Albert Schweitzer, Mother Teresa, Martin Luther King, come to mind. These people served to attain first place. And they seasoned all the world with their stewardship. They made a difference.

(2) "Have salt in yourselves, and be at peace with one another" (Mk 9:50b NRSV). I am going to interpret; you check me to see if l am in line with the sense of the Scripture. I think Jesus is telling us not to compete with each other in God's service. Remember this text started with the disciples arguing with each other about who was the greatest. Now Jesus is telling them and us to serve him in a way that keeps us from unhealthy competition. The Church has yet to learn the lesson. The competition between churches (and between the egos of competing preachers) is an embarrassment to this ideal. But that is another lesson.

Are You Possessed by Your Possessions?

Mark 10:13-31

Originally published March 13, 1994

Introduction

Today's question is down-to-earth and practical. And your people will under-stand this lesson. It does not follow they will truly agree with what Jesus said, but they will take in this teaching. This question hits us where we live. The text breaks down like this:

(1) The Child, 19:13-16.
(2) The Rich Man, 10:17-22.
(3) The Principle, 10:23-27.
(4) The Rewards, 10:28-31.

It seems to me the sense of the lesson is carried in parts two and three. I will comment on all four parts, but I would warn you that to teach all four parts will take more time than most of you will have. We mess up more sermons and lessons by trying to pack in too much than by having too little.

I. Receiving the Kingdom of God as a Child, 10:13-16.

Several times Jesus used the child as a backdrop to make a powerful idea. Last Sunday's lesson twice referred to the child (see Mk 9:36-37 and 9:42-48). Of course Jesus was open to children. And quite naturally parents wanted a blessing from Jesus on their children. And equally obviously, the disciples were mistaken in trying to keep the children from him. All of this you know and your class members know it too.

But what does Jesus mean when he said, "Whoever does not receive the kingdom of God as a little child will never enter it" (Mk 10:15 NRSV)? There is no place in the teachings of Jesus where he explains exactly what he means when he says we can't get into the kingdom of God except we become as a child. All the commentators have to guess what Jesus meant. And I have to guess too. Now that you know I am giving you my best thoughts, you will surely check these thoughts against your own. Here is what I think this might mean:

(1) The child is unashamed of being dependent. The natural state of the child is dependence. But when we grow older we put away this dependence. The sign of maturity is becoming independent. There is a sense in which we are always dependent on God. We live by his grace, his Word, his gifts.

(2) The child is naturally trusting. This comment is the flipside of dependence. I do not recall worrying about getting my next meal as child. I knew my parents would provide (and this was in the middle of the Great Depression). I trusted. God wants our trust to the same measure we gave this assumed trust to our parents.

Much could be written on this paragraph, but the main question in this lesson is raised in a more direct way in the Rich Young Ruler and the principle Jesus made of that incident.

II. What Must I Do to Inherit Eternal Life? 10:17-22.

Often Jesus was tested and taunted. His questioners were hostile. There is no evidence this rich man was anything but sincere. How else can we understand, "Jesus, looking at him, loved him…" (Mk 10:21a NRSV)? And the question asked of Jesus was basic. "What must I do to inherit eternal life?" (Mk 10:17b NRSV). I don't think the rich man stated his question the wrong way. Some commentators offer the opinion that the rich man was trying to earn his way to heaven. I take it the question was innocently framed; the man meant what he said. He wanted to know what he had to do to go to heaven.

Jesus asked the rich man if he had kept the basic law, and the rich man said he had. He was a good, moral man. So, we are not dealing with a fellow who has to put away some wicked pattern. There were no secret sins.

I wonder how Jesus saw through the rich man. But with that extra sense Jesus had about human nature, somehow he recognized and spoke to the one part of this fellow that needed amendment. Jesus said, "You lack one thing;

go, sell what you own, and give the money to the poor, and you will have treasure in heaven, then come, follow me" (Mk 10:21b NRSV).

The rich man "was shocked" (Mk 10:22 NRSV). I suspect the man thought Jesus was going to line out some theological principles. Repent of your sins. Believe in me. Confess before your friends. Such theological shorthand is what we have reduced "inheriting eternal life" to. But Jesus was much more immediate. He made the way to heaven and the way to serious discipleship a special fit. This man's problem was that he loved his possessions too much. He did not hold them; they held him. I do not doubt the man wanted to follow Jesus. He just did not want to follow Jesus enough to give away all he had to do it. The end of the story is sad. "He…went away grieving, for he had many possessions" (Mk 10:22 NRSV).

I wonder if Jesus would look at each of us, carefully craft the exact condition for our becoming a part of the disciple band, and then put us to the test…as he did this rich man. If that be so then becoming a follower of Jesus is always measured to the greatest rival in our affections to our love for Jesus. For some the leaving of family might be the test. For others it would be giving up some addiction. For others it would be insensitivity.

Somehow Jesus would hand-tool the question and put it to us at the point of greatest stress. We would follow if we could break through, break our idols and follow Jesus. This is the only person asked to follow Jesus in all of Mark who did not do so. The man wanted to follow; he just didn't want eternal life that much. I suspect the same test would reduce the number of disciples in any congregation. This man was not asked to tithe (a test far beyond most of our membership). This man was asked to give it all away. His possessions must have been some part of his security. He would have lost his identity, for he was "the rich man." He would have given away all he had spent his years accumulating. He would have become dependent, and in his wealthy condition he was independent (he would have been like a child again). I don't know whether I could do what Jesus asked the rich man to do or not. Regularly I give a tithe and more, but to give away all my wife and I have garnered over forty years of marriage? I hope I could. And if things become pretty important to us, then probably what Jesus would ask of you and me is to give it all away.

III. How Hard It Will Be for Those Who Have Wealth to Enter the Kingdom of God, 10:23-27.

This paragraph needs some interpretation. It was the opinion of the Jews that the people who had wealth were wealthy because God had blessed them.

God would not have blessed them were they not good and acceptable to God. So, God chose good people to receive his blessings. So, people who had much were the favored of God. Numerous Old Testament passages come to mind to underline the Jewish line of thought. Abraham was faithful to God; at the end of his life he was a very wealthy man. Job was tested, but at the end of his life his faithfulness was rewarded. He is described at the end of Job being more wealthy than he was before he was tested (see Job 42:12 17).

Jesus stood Jewish orthodoxy on its ear. "It is easier for a camel to go through the eye of a needle than for someone who is rich to enter the kingdom of God" (Mk 10:25 NRSV). And why is this so? Let me offer some thoughts.

(1) Wealth takes on some of the functions of God. God is supposed to be our provider. But if you get enough money, you can take care of yourself. God is replaced. God is supposed to be our security. But if you have enough, you are secure. God is replaced again. God is supposed to be our glory (that which we are most proud of). But some wealthy people are more proud of what they have done and gathered than they are of God. Again, God is put down and assigned a secondary role.

(2) Wealth is subtle. I doubt anyone intends to put wealth before God. It happens quietly, slowly, probably not by design. But when tested, there comes a time when wealth has us more than we have wealth. We can't let go.

(3) Wealth is deeply spiritual. Stewardship is not something we need to talk about to fund the church. Stewardship is something we need to talk about to get people to heaven. Until we recognize that wealth is the modern equivalent of idolatry, we will not see the power and the demonic in it. Always Jesus asked people to break their dearest idol as the price of discipleship. I suspect were he with us today in our money world, Jesus would ask us to break our wealth idol…just as he asked the rich man.

But this paragraph ends on a hopeful note. When the disciples asked, "Who can be saved?", Jesus said, "For mortals it is impossible, but not for God; for God all things are possible" (Mk 10:26b-27 NRSV). When modern America is called to a discipleship that requires us to give away our wealth, some will. There are young people today who walk away from money and fame for service and discipleship. Keep these modern apostles before your class.

ARE YOU POSSESSED BY YOUR POSSESSIONS?   171

IV. Look, We Have Left Everything and Followed You, 10:28-31.

Peter must have been powerfully impressed by the drama of the rich man offering himself to Jesus and then backing away from the call to discipleship. And when Jesus explained how hard it was for rich people to go to heaven, Peter internalized every word. He seems to be asking Jesus, "Well, we've given up everything to follow; what's going to happen to us?" Jesus gives a straight answer:

(1) Everyone who has given up this world and possessions to follow Jesus will receive a reward. If there is anything that is reinforced by the New Testament it is this: God does keep score. Goodness will be rewarded. Don't give up on this idea. Sometimes in this world and always in the next, God will reward his own.

(2) God replaces (in his own way) anything we give up for his service. So, if we give up family, God will give us a new family. If we give up money, God will give his own kind of provision...and in abundance. The promise is this: "who will not receive a hundredfold now in this age..." (Mk 10:30 NRSV).

(3) God has his own way of measuring how he will reward us. "Many who are first will be last, and the last will be first" (Mk 10:31 NRSV). This same God who overturns so many of our orthodoxies, this God will reward us in his own time and in his own way. And it may have some surprises for us. People who seem to be certain to sit on the front seat in heaven, may be toward the balcony. And some unusual folks may be nearer the front than ever we would imagine. This is my homespun interpretation of that last verse.

Conclusion

Once again I want to return to an idea I put before you in the Introduction: dwell on points two and three. They are the heart of the text. They are the substance of the question that is this lesson. I hope you will make your mark on the main idea. And I offer this lesson with a prayer. It will be hard for your people to hear; therefore, it will be hard to teach. You know most of your people are going to find some way to dismiss the main idea of the text. How can you make that unbelievable idea take root in their conscience? That is the test for the teacher...and for me in this text.

Are You Great?

Mark 10:32-45

ORIGINALLY PUBLISHED MARCH 20, 1994

Introduction

Jesus has finished the popular part of his ministry; he is leading the disciples toward Jerusalem. Jesus knows and he is trying to tell the disciples he is going to be crucified. Given the slowness of the apostles to understand Kingdom values, it is amazing to me to see the constant confidence Jesus had in them. In a matter of weeks Jesus would go back to his Heavenly Father. The teachings he came to put in the minds of the twelve were so shallow of root. But Jesus pressed on. He not only was obedient to death for our salvation; he was equally committed to the ability of the disciples/apostles to pick up where he would leave off. And so again and again he would teach and illustrate and underline and mark out what it meant to become a Kingdom person. Today's lesson will make the point again that getting culture and bad religion and ambition and just plain sin out of the system—that cleansing does not come easy. Anybody who says salvation is simple does not know much about the nature of sin or about our reluctance to put away the old person and become like Jesus. It is a long, slow, tedious process. Jesus had an infinite patience with his slow learners. I hope he has the same patience with us, his latter-day followers.

I. Reinforcing the Teaching about the Cross, 10:32-43.

Note the way our text begins: "They were on the road, going up to Jerusalem, and Jesus was walking ahead of them; they were amazed, and those who followed were afraid" (Mk 10:32a NRSV). Two ideas come out of this opening.

(1) Jesus was ultimately alone. The disciples were protective and they cared for Jesus with a great love. But they did not and could not understand. Only after the cross and the resurrection would they put it all together. The teachings that had been so dense and vague and strange—well, after the cross/resurrection the words of Jesus and the deeds of Jesus would make plain what had been absolutely incomprehensible before. So, see the picture: Jesus "walking ahead of them." Alone. It was not just in the Garden of Gethsemane that Jesus was alone. He carried the weight, the dead weight, of the cross for a long time.

(2) The disciples were beginning to hear Jesus when he said he was going to Jerusalem to die. I don't think the twelve understood any theory of the atonement. They did not know all that was involved in God's design to effect our salvation. But so often had Jesus said he was going to Jerusalem to die until now they are beginning to take it in.

Why did Jesus take "the twelve aside again and began to tell them what was to happen to him"? (Mk 10:32b NRSV). First, Jesus wants to spare his followers pain. Second, Jesus wants them to begin "to process" what is happening to God's larger designs in his dying. The theology of the early church is being first thought in these sessions. And these ideas will have to mature in the light of the cross and resurrection. But they began in these first classes with the twelve. Understanding who Jesus was and what he came to do were not instant revelations for the Church. If Paul had to mature his thinking for ten, twenty years before they came to us in his letters, how much more did the twelve have to think through what they were experiencing? Later they would make theology, the theology we study today. It all started with Jesus getting them ready for the cross. Afterward they would explain the cross.

II. The Request of James and John, 10:35-40.

Usually we associate Peter, James, and John as a special trio among the twelve. At the Transfiguration it was Peter, James, and John who were witnesses (see Mk 9:2-8). And the same trinity were present in the Garden during an agonizing time (see Mt 26:37). Since Jesus drew these three especially close, we could assume these three also "understood" Jesus best. But this text proves that theory wrong.

James and John tried to snare Jesus with words. "Teacher, we want you to do for us whatever we ask of you" (Mk 10:35b NRSV). Jesus would have none of it. Before he would consent to such, he wanted to know what would follow. Then they dropped it on him: "Grant us to sit, one at your right hand and one at your left, in your glory" (Mk 20:37 NRSV). Old ideas die hard. Jesus had been telling these people for three years that he did not come to set up a worldly kingdom, but so deeply ingrained in the disciples was the idea of the kind of leader the Messiah would be until even when they got it straight that Jesus really was the Messiah, they could not get it straight what kind of Messiah he would be. They were still trying to put him into the mold of Jewish expectation. It would be a physical, worldly, powerful kingdom. There would have to be assistants and there would be power to be shared. And there would be fame and notoriety. And if all these were to be spread around, James and John wanted their full share. So, they put aside any reservation, went straight to Jesus and asked for a prominent place.

At this point, I could heap shame on James and John. But if James and John could follow Jesus for three years, witness all Jesus had done, listen to all he had taught and still be so far from understanding the ways of Jesus, does it not follow that you and I may be a long way from really understanding Jesus, too? Think about that before you tar the disciples too much in this lesson.

Jesus turned their request. He took them seriously. If they really wanted a prominent place in the Kingdom of God, they were going to have to "drink the cup that I drink" and "be baptized with the baptism that I am baptized with" (Mk 20:38 NRSV). Let me make a suggestion about what "drink the cup that I drink" and "be baptized with the baptism that I am baptized with" means. I think these phrases mean that James and John, if they want to have real leadership in Christ's Kingdom, will have to live out the Jesus kind of life. They will be misunderstood like Jesus. They will be harassed and persecuted like Jesus. They will suffer like Jesus. And they will come to great leadership out of great service/suffering.

James and John did not get the grant they asked. Jesus denied them. "To sit at my right hand or at my left is not mine to grant, but is for those for whom it has been prepared" (Mk 10:40 NRSV). Real leadership in Christ's Kingdom is never given; it is earned in humble service. Sometimes it is earned in dangerous service.

III. Jealousy and Teaching, 10:41-45.

Of course the ten heard about the request of the brothers, and the ten were angry. They were jealous. Maybe Jesus would give the brothers what they asked because they asked first. The fears of the ten were misplaced. And the real danger in this situation was that the bond of the twelve could be broken. They could fall on each other and the group could disintegrate. "So Jesus called them and said to them, 'You know that among the Gentiles those whom they recognize as their rulers lord it over them.... But it is not so among you; but whoever wishes to become great among you must be your servant, and whoever wishes to be first among you must be slave of all' " (Mk 10:42-44 NRSV).

Jesus was different. If you want to be rich in the Kingdom of heaven, you are to give away what you have to the poor. If you want to be great, you are the greatest servant. If you want to save your life, you risk it. If you hold onto your life, you will surely lose it. These are some of the radical ideas Jesus taught (and there were more; see Mt 5:21-48). The trouble with commentators like me is that we usually take the hard sayings of Jesus and tone them down. We tame Jesus. The visionary Jesus is made to be the practical Jesus. By smooth theology we pull the teeth from the sharp bites he makes in normal patterns of living. Jesus was different. Jesus was so different he would be deemed impractical in the boardrooms of most seminaries who are founded to teach his words. Jesus is radical; he would not pass muster in the average deacons meeting. He is too "far out."

But here is the teaching. If you want to get to the top you must do the humble service of the one who is at the bottom. The Church ought to be set up this way. It isn't, and the cause of Jesus is the poorer for it. Tell the people we don't make Jesus out-of-touch and radical when we take him straight. We make the Kingdom attractive to people who are longing for the Jesus who really did serve more than anyone else and love more and risk more. And therefore, he is elevated higher than anyone else. That is what Paul meant when he wrote:

Let the same mind be in you that was in Christ Jesus, who, though he was in the form of God, did not regard equality with God as something to be exploited, but emptied himself, taking the form of a slave, being born in human likeness. And being found in human form, he humbled himself and became obedient to the point of death even the death of a cross. Therefore God also highly exalted him and gave him the name that is above every name, so that at the name of Jesus every knee should bend, in heaven and on earth and under the earth, and every tongue should confess that Jesus Christ is Lord, to the glory of God the Father. (Phil 2:5-11 NRSV)

Paul was not with the twelve when Jesus gave the teaching that is our text. But Paul got the message. And Paul saw clearly that Jesus did not just teach humility and service. He acted it out. So, the reason Jesus has come to such place in the Church is because he first was willing to spend himself fully.

Read again Paul's words on Jesus. Jesus was our example of "whoever wishes to become great among you must be your servant" (Mk 10:43 NRSV). Once in a great while the Church is blessed with a saint who takes this text literally. Always these saints are first thought to be strange, a little crazy. But time passes. Then we see them for what they are. They are the real disciples, and the rest of us are only imitations of the real thing.

Are You Obedient in Little Things?

Mark 11:1-11

ORIGINALLY PUBLISHED MARCH 27, 1994

Introduction

I would never have chosen this text for a lesson. I would have overlooked the "little things" (and that is what the lesson is about) and hurried on to the story of Jesus' triumphal entry into Jerusalem. But now that I've been assigned this text, I've discovered a part of the Gospel that until this study I had overlooked. I'm now glad this text was chosen, for I think I see meaning in what until this time had been a filler passage in Mark's Gospel.

There was a time when I was a careless student. Then I changed and became a careful student. When I was a careless student I usually received grades that were B's and C's. Then when I changed I usually received A's. What was the difference? Was I all of a sudden more intelligent? Not really. The intelligence was constant. The difference was "little things." As a casual student I would slap at the outline of the professor; commit a little to memory and let the rest go. When I became a careful student I learned all the material...and I learned the detail. I studied until I got it all. I stayed with it until I got it right. And the difference was a dramatic improvement. I learned more; I graded higher. And the difference? Little things.

This lesson is about obedience in little things. Stay with me through the development of the text. I found more than I expected.

I. Jesus Was Careful in Little Things, 11 :1-7.

Jesus was approaching Jerusalem and the final days of his ministry. Since the conversation with the disciples at Caesarea Philippi (Mk 8:27-30) Jesus has been facing toward and leading his disciples toward Jerusalem, betrayal and death. Now the end of the road nears. By way of Jericho and from the east they climb the steep range of hills. Jerusalem sits atop the ridge. So, the little band comes first to Bethany then Bethphage (Mark has the two reversed). And at this point Jesus stopped.

Now for a digression. Were you to see Jesus only through the eyes of Mark's Gospel, you could conclude that Jesus was only rarely in Jerusalem. But John's Gospel gives a different picture. Often Jesus was in and around the Holy City. He attended the religious feasts. He was often teaching at the temple. And it was over Jerusalem that he grieved. "Jerusalem, Jerusalem! … How often have I desired to gather your children together as a hen gathers her brood under her wings, and you were not willing! See, your house is left to you, desolate" (Mt 23:37-38 NRSV). I make this point to emphasize that Jesus knew his way around Jerusalem.

Now the plan unfolds. "He sent two of his disciples and said to them, 'Go into the village ahead of you, and immediately as you enter it, you will find tied there a colt…' " (Mk 11:2 NRSV). And then in detail Jesus spells out what the disciples will find, what they are to say and what they are to bring back from the errand. Note the little things:

- "Go into the village ahead of you" (they were to go to a precise place.)
- "Immediately as you enter it, you will find there a colt that has never been ridden" (only a certain kind of colt meets that description).
- "Untie it and bring it" (the point of errand is to get a specific colt, one who has never been ridden).
- "If anyone says to you, 'Why are you doing this?' just say this, 'The Lord needs it and will send it back here immediately' " (the lines were to be memorized by the visiting disciples; the instructions were explicit).
- "Some bystanders said to them, 'What are you doing, untying the colt?' They told them what Jesus had said; and they allow them to take it" (It all worked out just like Jesus said it would; nothing was left to chance. Nothing went wrong). At this point we can put the emphasis on the obedience of the disciples or we can put the search light on the detailed plan of Jesus. I think the greater place should be given the plan. You see, I think Jesus was being more obedient in little things than the disciples were. God had sent Jesus to do something profoundly important. Soon he would die

on the cross to save us from our sins. What Jesus was doing was working through every little detail of the things the Messiah was promised to do. He was self-consciously in step with the Old Testament. He was living up to and acting the part of the one who would come and be the clearest and best revelation of the will of God, the best revelation of the love of God.

Should we turn this lesson to the obedience of the disciples I think we would miss the larger message. So, I am grateful the disciples were exact in their obedience. But the larger obedience was the Christ who was keeping faith with all the prophets had said he would be.

II. Little Things Mark a Trail for Us, 11:7-11.

Buried back in the Old Testament is a verse that tells how Jesus was supposed to enter Jerusalem before his crucifixion. We are not nearly as familiar with the Old Testament as we need to be. Were it known to us as it was known to Jesus, we would see more design in the ways and words of Jesus than we do. Listen to this prophetic worship from Zechariah:

> Rejoice greatly, O daughter Zion!
> Shout aloud, O daughter Jerusalem!
> Lo, your king comes to you;
> triumphant and victorious is he,
> humble and riding on a donkey,
> on a colt, the foal of a donkey. (Zech 9:9 NRSV)

If Jesus were the Messiah, he would be required to act out the prophecy of Zechariah. We take such Old Testament prophecies as being out-of-touch with anything we need to know. Jesus didn't dismiss them. He fulfilled them. So, if he were the Messiah as the disciples had said he was (see Mk 8:29), then he had to stay in touch with what the Old Testament said the Messiah would be. Now many of the messianic promises were kept in ways that were different from Jewish expectation, but that is not the point. The main idea, the strong idea is that they were kept. The "little things" were not allowed to fall away. Jesus really was a Jewish Messiah who lived up to the promises of the Jewish prophets who foretold his coming.

Years after when Paul was writing theology for the Church, this old Pharisee would remember all those Old Testament promises. And one by one Jesus had kept them. He was marking a trail for us. He was not just letting the disciples who walked with him and worked with him know he was the Messiah. He was marking a trail for the Church so that we could know who he was too. So, the kind of colt he rode into Jerusalem was foretold. The words he would say on the cross were predicted, and the prediction was fulfilled. The kind of tomb he would be laid in was predicted, and the prediction came true. And on and on the detail goes. Jesus did all the little things that would let us know beyond a shadow of a doubt that he thought he was the Messiah. And he wanted the Church to get it right. The clues were in the little things. And Jesus got the little things right. He was obedient to what God sent him to do.

III. An Obedient Christ Needs Obedient Disciples.

In Matthew's Gospel, there is a teaching we need to put along side our text of the day. It reads like this: "A disciple is not above the teacher, nor a slave above the master; it is enough for the disciple to be like the teacher, and the slave like the master" (Mt 10:24-25a NRSV) The key words are, "it is enough for the disciple to be like the teacher."

The larger sense of this text is that Jesus was exceedingly careful to fulfill the smallest detail. He was obedient in the little things. In so doing he kept the promises made about him and he marked the trail for the Church when they would write the theology that would define who Jesus was and what he came to do. The small story in this text is that two disciples were careful to obey what Jesus told them. The implied teaching is that if we are to follow Jesus we must be as care as were the two who were sent for the colt. The strong teaching is that all who follow Jesus must give heed to the little things.

In the Introduction to this lesson I told you about a transformation I made when I was a college student from casual to careful, from mindless of the little things to mindful of them. And it changed everything. Literally it changed my life. The real application of this lesson is an appeal to the careless Christian to become a careful one.

The Church and the gospel and the witness and the reputation of even Christ himself is made small by that carelessness in little things. I'm not sure many of us are into much that is really big. My life is in the little things. But that does not make me small; rather, it defines the little things as more important than ever we know. The rearing of a child is a million little things. The gathering of a Church is a million little things. Excellence in ministry is attention to detail. Clean, sharp performance on the piano is attention to the little things...getting them right. And that's what ministry is, too. A thousand times a we the little things come up to be our opportunity or they come up to be our undoing. The gentle word. The encouraging greeting. The forgiveness given. The honest answer...given in kindness. The witness spoken at just the right time. And on and on. These are the little things. And they are the difference.

Over in Matthew there is the story of the three stewards. You remember those fellows. One was given five talents; another was given two, and the last was given one. When it was all done and the master had gone away and then come back, here is the commendation, he gave one of the faithful stewards, "And the one with the two talents also came forward, saying, 'Master, you handed over to me two talents; see, I have made two more talents.' His master said to him, 'Well done, good and trustworthy slave; you have been trustworthy in a few things, I will put you in charge of many things' " (Mt 25:22-23 NRSV). If we get the little things right it is the way of Jesus to entrust us with larger things. But not until we are faithful in the little things.

The Role of the Servant

Mark 12:1-12

ORIGINALLY PUBLISHED OCTOBER 4, 1998

Introduction

Today's parable is written in bold strokes. The sum of the Gospel is in it.

• God is the owner of the vineyard. God trusts his vineyard "to tenants" (12:1b).
• In due time, the owner asks for a return on his investment. He sends messengers to the tenants asking his part of the income. These messengers are the Old Testament prophets. The messengers were treated badly; no produce or income was sent to the owner.
• The owner reasoned that the unruly tenants would respect his "beloved son" (12:6). But the owner's trust was misplaced. Instead of respecting the son, they reasoned the vineyard would be theirs if they killed the son. So they did (12:7-8). Jesus was the "beloved son." The tenants were the people God had trusted…the Jews.
• What had been trusted to the Jews has been given to the Church.
• The One rejected (Jesus) has become the cornerstone of the Church. The One they crucified is the very One the Church worships. This parable is almost a condensation of the Bible. What is the meaning of the parable for us today? How do we tell the story and recover the power the early Church felt in it? That's our challenge.

I. Stewardship, 12:1-8.

The identification of Israel as "the tenants" in the story needs clarification. "A man planted a vineyard, put a fence around it, dug a pit for the wine press, and built a watchtower; then he leased it to tenants and went to another country" (12:1b). Here's the way George A. Buttrick explains the tie between Israel and "the tenants":

> Every gift had been lavished, every preparation made, that it might "bring forth abundantly." The reference is clearly to Israel. Israel had been "planted." She had been taught the worship of the one God while other nations were still immersed in polytheistic barbarism; she had been blessed in singers whose psalms have since become the world's confessional and hymnary; she had been "hedged about" by prophetic warnings, harrowed by persecutions, and fertilized by countless mercies (Buttrick, *The Parables of Jesus* [New York: Harper and Brothers Publishers, 1928], 213-214).

The most powerful idea in this parable is failed stewardship. "The tenants" had been given much and much was entrusted to them. Most of all, "the tenants" were given freedom. God trusted them. God did not give the tenants the vineyard, God asked them to care for it. As always, there is accountability in the owner-tenant relationship. But often when God trusts us with a job and gives us some time and space to do it, we misread the situation. We think because God gives us time and space, God has stopped being the owner. What begins as stewardship quietly becomes ownership. Halford E. Luccock wrote of this parable, "It depicts the subtle way in which men reject their status as trustees, and come to think of themselves as outright owners, with the 'absentee landlord' forgotten" (Luccock, *The Interpreter's Bible*, vol. 7 [New York: Abingdon Press, 1951], 837).

We usually define "stewardship" as the giving of money. That is certainly one of its meanings and there is a time when the stewardship of money should be stressed. But this parable is about stewardship written large. God has entrusted us with a part of God's vineyard. With a trust that flatters us all, God has stepped back to let us make the most of our lives in God's service.

For millions of Americans who were reared in the church, life that began in stewardship has become a race to see who can gather the most stuff. In the near-mad race to be an American success we have forgotten the terms of the original contract. We are in danger of confusing stewardship and ownership. This parable is a wake-up call.

The subtle shift from stewardship to ownership is something I've known. For more than twenty years I was honored to serve as pastor of First Baptist Church of Asheville, North Carolina. It was a stewardship. But with the passing years I came to speak of "my church." I did not mean evil when I spoke so. It seemed natural. After all, I was responsible. Probably in ways I was not aware I acted as if the church were mine. But it never was. The church belonged to the people. In a larger sense, the church belonged to Christ. And sometimes I spoke of it as "my church." What a foolishness! There came a day when my fantasy about "my church" was dashed. I went to another church. And the old First Church went right on. I was not essential for her health.

It was never mine. I was a steward for a season. My picture is on the wall beside all those preachers who served for a time. What I once thoughtlessly claimed as mine has been given to other able hands. Confusing stewardship and ownership is easy to do. I've done it.

II. Rejection, 12:9-11.

As the story unfolds, surly tenants rebuff servants sent by the vineyard owner. Then he sends his son. The tenants are so corrupt that they see the son's coming as an opportunity. If they kill him, then the vineyard will be theirs. The owner will no longer have an heir (12:7). "So they seized him, killed him, and threw him out of the vineyard" (12:8).

"What then will the owner of the vineyard do? He will come and destroy the tenants and give the vineyard to others" (12:9). Then follows a clever turn of phrase in this story.

• Most people think Jesus was rejected. He was crucified, humiliated, hung on a tree. Surely that is rejection.
• But ultimately it was not Jesus who was rejected. It was a soul-dead orthodoxy that could not recognize the Messiah when he came. The trust given to Abraham (Gen 12:1-3) and confirmed at Sinai in covenant was withdrawn.

Sometimes people think that when we reject God we put God in a bind. If God doesn't get our services, God will go begging. But that's not the way things are.

• Rejecting God's service does the rejecter more harm than it does God. It is arrogant to think God can't make it without us. When we think straight, we see that our lives are given dignity by the invitation to God's service. The Kingdom does not hang by the slender thread of our talent or willingness to serve.

• God has a pattern of taking the humble, the seemingly insignificant people of the Kingdom, and trusting them with service. For example, once great mainline denominations called America to Christ. Now it is groups who were unknown just a few decades ago. Luccock put it this way: "When his call to evangelize the world came to the deaf ears of archbishops, it was heard by a cobbler, William Carey" (*The Interpreter's Bible*, vol. 7, 838).

The tenants thought they were rejecting the Owner. Ultimately, it was the tenants who were rejected and cast away. God has entrusted us to keep God's vineyard. That's wonderful if we remember our stewardship. It's a dreadful thing if we fail. This text breathes accountability. God really does expect productivity. To use an expression all Americans understand: God expects a return on God's investment. This is a tougher Gospel than most of us know.

III. Communication, 12:12.

"When they realized that he had told this parable against them…" (12:12a). This sentence contains two strong ideas:

• Jesus could communicate. Jesus spoke in words common people understood. Jesus identified himself as the "beloved son." He was more than a servant; he was God's Son. It doesn't get much plainer than that. In our parable, Jesus summarized Israel's history. God had given them special treatment and enormous trust. They had mishandled the prophets, and he correctly predicted they would kill the owner of the vineyard's son. Jesus had the big picture. He told it straight.
• The religious leaders were not dumb; they got the point. Jesus took a swing at them with this story. He hit them, and they knew it. If Jewish leadership had their way, they would have arrested Jesus on the spot. "But they feared the crowd. So they left him and went away" (12:12b).

Looking back, it seems that one of the religious leaders should have said, "He's got it right. We need to take this pointed parable to heart and change. Our religion is turned inward. We need to do what Jonah reluctantly did. Let's stop counting temple tax and start counting hurting people. Let's do different and better." But even in the presence of Jesus, these people were locked in, and closed-minded. They heard what Jesus said, but it did not make hearts tender. What a pity.

The title to our lesson is "The Role of the Servant." This parable tells us we will serve or be cast away. In my comment I've tied the lesson to history, but this lesson is more than history. This lesson is living, current truth. God has entrusted to us a piece of God's vineyard for the brief time we are on this earth. Our station before God depends on the way we perform. Other parables tell of faithful stewards and happy endings. "Well done, good slave! Because you have been trustworthy in a very small thing, take charge of ten cities" (Lk 19:17). The end of the story doesn't have to turn out bad. I earnestly pray I will be numbered among those servants who are found faithful.

Waiting for the Good News

Mark 13:24-37

ORIGINALLY PUBLISHED NOVEMBER 28, 1999

Introduction

Mark 13 is a difficult assignment. It seems Mark has condensed Jesus' sayings on Last Things, put them together, and flung them at us. Actually, what Mark did makes good sense.

(1) Mark 13 is about more than the Second Coming of Christ. William Barclay did an excellent job of separating the strands of thought in the chapter. He lists five:
- Prophecies of destruction of Jerusalem, 13:1-2 and 14-20.
- Warnings of persecution to come, 13:9-13.
- Warnings of dangers of last days, 13:3-6 and 21-22.
- Warnings of Second Coming, 13:7 8 and 24-27.
- Warnings of necessity to be on watch, 13:28-37. (*The Gospel of Mark* [Philadelphia: Westminster Press, 1956], 320-321)

Our assignment concerns the last two parts Barclay listed.

(2) Chapter 13 requires some knowledge of Hebrew history to interpret it appropriately. Jews believed deeply that they were God's chosen. But history was not kind to them. How could Jews be chosen when they were being enslaved and oppressed by the Babylonians, Greeks, Romans? They were scattered all over the world. If they were favored, God certainly had a strange way of showing it. But events had not discouraged the Jews. They believed God would intervene in history. Jews would be gathered, honored, and elevated.

(3) Keeping the Fall of Jerusalem in AD 70 and the Second Coming of Christ separate is not easy in this text. The shift from one to the other is abrupt in some places.

Today is the first Sunday of Advent. But our text is not about the coming of baby Jesus. He has already come. This lesson is about another coming, a Second Coming cloaked in mystery. The early Church lived for the Second Coming. They hoped, prayed, and dreamed of it. To catch some of that long-lost expectation, hear Paul's word to the Corinthians, "so that you are not lacking in any spiritual gift as you wait for the revealing of our Lord Jesus Christ" (1 Cor 1:7).

In these days that lively expectation is gone. Halford E. Luccock wrote of the Second Coming, "Its essence was something deeper: the faith that God is a factor in the world, today and tomorrow; that he will act redeemingly in human history; that the conquest of evil comes not of our wit and muscle, but of his continuing sovereignty" (*The Interpreter's Bible*, vol. 7 [New York: Abingdon Press, 1951], 863). Our hope is in God—not science or education. Although I am invested in both, I know that lasting, final hope lies in God. This lesson is striking at our idolatry. We have good news. God has moved among us once in the baby Jesus, and God will make another move with that same Jesus. When the Church is sharp to its task, it is "waiting for the good news" of Jesus' return. Don't pretend to prepare for Jesus, but instead, teach about when the God of love and justice will settle up with us all.

I. Jesus Predicts the Second Coming, 13:7-8 and 24-27.

I preach only occasionally on the Second Coming. I suspect most of you are a lot like me. You teach this doctrine when it is assigned. The end effect of what you and I are doing is to marginalize the Second Coming in the ministry of the Church.

There are good reasons for the way we act. It is not unbelief; our hesitancy comes from another quarter.

(1) No one knows much about the Second Coming. We can speak much more confidently about lying, cheating, forgiveness, and grace. We know what the Bible says about those things.

(2) The people who have reached out and claimed the Second Coming as a theme for their preaching and teaching often are not people we admire. They leave whole sections of the gospel unspoken, while they speak dogmatically about things they know little about. And they've often been wrong.

(3) Most important of all, it has been nearly two thousand years since Jesus went back to heaven. How long can we expect people to stay on the edges of their chairs anticipating, waiting, and watching? It's been seventy-five generations since Jesus lived. A kind of "expectancy fatigue" has overtaken the larger part of the Church; therefore, most of us are silent about the Second Coming. We don't say we don't believe in it; we just don't say anything at all.

Where did we get the idea of the Second Coming? Mark said: "Then they will see 'the Son of Man coming in clouds' with great power and glory" (13:26). In John 14:1-3, Jesus says the same thing, only using different language. Luke affirms the Second Coming when he describes the ascension of Jesus. Two men in white robes said, "Men of Galilee, why do you stand looking up toward heaven? This Jesus, who has been taken up from you into heaven, will come in the same way as you saw him go into heaven" (Acts 1:11). We may have marginalized the teaching, but the Gospel writers didn't.

Jesus said he would come again. Three ideas we need to note:

(1) There will be signs before he comes. Wars, earthquakes, and famines are listed in 13:7-8. The natural order will be disturbed. "The sun will be darkened…the moon will not give light…stars will be falling from heaven…" (13:24-25). The trouble with these signs is that they occur all the time. I've lived through a number of wars. I've read about earthquakes all my life. And famines have come and gone for centuries. This does not discredit what Jesus said; it makes it hard to fix a particular war, earthquake, famine and say, "This is a sign the Last Days are upon us."

(2) Jesus will "come with great power and glory" (13:26b). Trying to imagine this scene is both awesome and intimidating. Should I be alive at that time, I am sure I would be simultaneously scared, amazed, and delighted. For centuries saints have been buried in a graveyard east of Jerusalem. They are buried there because they believe Jesus is going to come back to the same place from which he ascended. The Apostle Paul spoke of resurrection day like this: "All die in Adam, so all will be made alive in Christ. But each in his own order: Christ the first fruits, then at his coming those who belong to Christ" (1 Cor 15:22-23). When Jesus came the first time, he was a tiny baby. He quietly slipped into this world. When he comes again, it will be triumphant. "In the clouds with great power and glory" means he will not go unnoticed.

(3) Special attention will be given to "the elect" (13:27). They will be gathered "from the four winds, from the ends of the earth to the ends of heaven" (13:27b). These elect are all the saints from all nations, all of whom belong to Christ.

Jesus predicted he would come again. "A number of passages …demonstrate that Jesus is a true prophet. The certainty with which he foresaw events that are now past should encourage readers to have confidence in his words about the future" (Pheme Perkins, *The New Interpreter's Bible*, vol. 8 [Nashville: Abingdon Press, 1995], 685). Since Jesus has been right about so many things he predicted, we should not dismiss what he said about the Second Coming.

II. Perceptive People May Be Able to Anticipate It, 13:28-30.

Mark 13 began with amazed disciples discussing the impressive size of the temple stones. "Most of them were 37 feet long, 18 feet wide, and 12 feet thick" (*Oxford Annotated Bible* [New York: Oxford University Press, 1991], 68 NT). That's big! Jesus' response to country boys who were gaping at city buildings was this: "Do you see these great buildings? Not one stone will be left here upon another; all will be thrown down" (13:2).

The disciples could not get it out of their minds. Jesus said the beautiful, enormous temple would be torn down. The company walked out of Jerusalem, across a brook, and up the Mount of Olives. They sat down for a rest. The crowds had not followed them; it was a relatively sane, quiet moment. Looking across the little valley they saw Jerusalem on the hill opposite them. The temple in all its glory was right before their eyes. One of the disciples decided this was the right time to learn more about the prediction of Jesus that the temple would be dismantled, torn down.

"Tell us, when will this be, and what will be the sign that all these things are about to be accomplished?" (13:4). The disciples wanted to know when. When will the temple be destroyed? When will the Second Coming be? We all want Jesus to point to a date on the calendar.

I suspect he turned to a fig tree nearby; the Mount of Olives still has figs and olives. It was Passover time; that means it would have been spring. "From the fig tree learn its lesson: as soon as its branch becomes tender and puts forth its leaves, you know that summer is near" (13:28). My maternal grandfather was a farmer; all his life he lived on the land and became a student of nature and the seasons. He could name every tree; he knew the sequence of bud and bloom in springtime. He had no weather forecaster to tell him what tomorrow's weather would be, yet he knew an east wind meant rain was likely, a green cloud meant hail. He watched, and stayed alert.

If a farmer can become so aware of the signs of nature, can a Christian not become aware of the ways of God? If the answer to the above question is yes (and I believe it is), shouldn't we become sensitive to what God is doing? And again, the answer is yes.

For a long time, people have guessed about the Second Coming. Jesus said three things we need to note:

(1) Perceptive saints can "get onto" God's timetable. You may be one of them. When we are really attuned to God's ways, we come to anticipate God's movements.

(2) "This generation will not pass away until all these things have taken place" refers to the Fall of Jerusalem. It happened in AD 70, and when it was over, "not one stone" was left upon another. It was a ghastly, brutal scene.

(3) Jesus was sure of himself. "Heaven and earth will pass away, but my words will not pass away" (13:31). He was the Messiah; he was also a prophet. Much of what he predicted has already come to pass; I have confidence the rest will come in God's good time.

III. Don't Fret the Details; Be Ready, 13:31-37.

The chapter ends with clear words on an unclear subject.

(1) Don't consume yourselves with trying to figure it out. "But about that day or hour no one knows, neither the angels in heaven, nor the Son, but only the Father" (13:32). If Jesus doesn't know when the Second Coming is going to be, we surely cannot predict it. But this text suggests more. Trying to figure out the time of the Second Coming is not something to worry about.

(2) Our text repeats the important thing. "Keep awake.... And what I say to you I say to all: Keep awake" (13:35a and 37). Being alert for every sign of the Second Coming misses the point. Halford E. Luccock got the sense of it in this marvelous instruction:

> The word "watch" reaches into the whole spread of life. Someone has said
> that the worst "ism" in the world is...somnambulism. There are so many

forms of sleepwalking—the glazed eyes, which never notice that one's
ideals are being whittled away, one's purposes being pared down; never
notice the evil forces in the world, gaining strength. Watch and pray
against the sin that so easily trips us up, the compromise with wrong, so
reasonable in the beginning, so deadly in the end. Watch, lest we neglect
the renewal of life in communion with God, let our sympathies harden.
Watch, lest the great opportunities for service to God's kingdom come and
pass by, unseen and unseized. (*The Interpreter's Bible*, 865)

We are God's servants. Doing God's will and work should consume our
lives. If we are doing the job right, the Second Coming will not be a threat,
nor will we be caught off guard. Live straight every day. Do what is right,
and do it with a willing heart. If the Second Coming interrupts us, good!
God is in control; everything will be all right. And should we die (as our parents and grandparents before us) before the Second Coming, in a very
personal way Jesus will have made a special trip for us. And that will be fine
too. In the meantime, we are doing God's work and "waiting for the good
news."

⁓

Resurrection and Life

Mark 16:1-8

ORIGINALLY PUBLISHED APRIL 20, 2003

Introduction

There is a rough realism about Mark's Gospel. Jesus died wondering if God had forsaken him (15:34), and the women who heard the good news about resurrection "fled from the tomb, for terror and amazement had seized them; and they said nothing to anyone, for they were afraid" (16:8). That's the end. It is abrupt and suggests it is unfinished. What are we to make of this?

Our text (Mk 16:1-8) is the real ending of Mark. I have read no commentator who thinks otherwise. Mark 16:9-20 is usually called "the longer ending of Mark." It was added probably early in the second century. I remember how unsettling it was to me when first I learned about the textual variations in the Bible. It seemed to border on saying that the Bible was not true as it appears. I had some faithful teachers who helped me. They did not teach me to believe the Bible was not true; they helped me see how it was written, assembled, and handed down to us through the hands of numerous translators. If you are like me, reared to reverence the Scripture, you want to defend the Bible and you want to be intellectually honest. Bible scholars are still trying to sort through well-intentioned additions and "corrections" made by those who gathered New Testament documents, edited them, and decided which ones would be included. That process took about 300 years. The goal of these scholars is to find the true text written by the inspired writers. That's the reason Mark 16:9-20 is called "the longer ending of Mark." Mark did not write it; we don't know who did. Our text stops at 16:8

because that's the last line we are sure Mark wrote. A part of Mark's ending may be lost.

The condition of the text does not confuse Mark's meaning. We know what he intended to say. "He has been raised; he is not here" is the point and to the point (16:6b). That terse message changes everything.

I. Sorting Out the Details.

You know how modern Americans bury their dead. But the death of Jesus took place a long time ago and in a very different culture. Here are some details that will make the more important parts of the session clear:

(1) "When the sabbath was over" (16:1a). That would be Saturday at sundown. Notice how the nearest followers of Jesus still observed Jewish law.

(2) "Mary Magdalene, and Mary the mother of James and Salome" (16:1b). These two women were among the inner group of followers. They are named twice because their story is bedrock to confirmation of the resurrection (see 15:47 and 16:1b).

(3) "Bought spices, so that they might go and anoint him" (16:1c). Joseph of Arimathea wrapped the body of Jesus in a "linen cloth" and laid him "in a tomb that had been hewn out of rock" (15:46). Apparently, late Friday afternoon the body was taken down from the cross, wrapped in the linen cloth, and rushed to burial. It all had to happen before sundown and Sabbath. Since the burial rites had not been completed on Friday, they would be completed on Sunday. The spices were perfumed oils to be rubbed on the body of the dead.

(4) "Very early on the first day of the week, when the sun had risen they went to the tomb" (16:2). John says before daylight; Mark says after "the sun had risen" (see Jn 20:1). Henry Turlington wrote, "Mark's meaning is something like this, 'As early the next morning as they possibly could' " (*The Broadman Bible Commentary*, vol. 8 [Nashville: Broadman Press, 1969], 400).

(5) "They had been saying to one another, 'Who will roll away the stone for us from the entrance to the tomb?' " (16:3). Tombs were carved out of rock. Sometimes tombs were large enough to hold several generations of a family. Since the stone at the entrance was large and very heavy, the tomb was probably a room carved out of soft stone. Shelves were made along the walls. Deceased family members were embalmed and placed on the shelves. The stone kept away grave robbers; it could be moved, but it would take several strong men to do it.

(6) "As they entered the tomb, they saw a young man, dressed in a white robe, sitting on the right side" (16:5). Think of the "young man" as an angel. As there were angels at the birth, so there were angels at the resurrection. What Jesus was doing on earth commanded the attention of heaven.

These details are not the meat of the text, but knowing the details helps us understand the message. The four Gospels differ in the details of the resurrection, but on the main thing they are agreed: Jesus was resurrected from the dead.

II. The State of Mind of the Women.

"When the sabbath was over, Mary Magdalene, and Mary the mother of James and Salome bought spices, so that they might go and anoint him" (16:1). This tells us all we need to know about what the women expected to find at the tomb. Jesus was dead. They loved him in life, and they wanted every decency for him in death. Probably these women had helped care for Jesus and the apostles in life (see Lk 8:1-3). From their resources they bought spices to anoint Jesus in death.

Jesus had predicted he would rise from the dead after three days (see Mk 8:31 for one account), but strangely this message was lost on those who followed him most closely. They were trapped in the moment, and their minds could not take in the idea of resurrection. When Jesus died on the cross, there is not a shred of evidence that the men who would later be apostles ever expected to see Jesus again. Like the women who went to the tomb on Sunday, they thought Jesus dead and buried.

This uniform state of mind of the women and the apostles is a witness to the truth of our Easter story. They were more than surprised; they were dumbfounded. They had missed the clear message Jesus had given them about the cross and resurrection; with the exception of a few women, they had been less than courageous at his death. Their idealistic time with Jesus was over. He was dead, and so was the dream they had when first they followed him. William Barclay said,

> One thing is certain—if Jesus had not risen from the dead we would never have heard of Him. The attitude of the women was that they had come to pay the last tribute to a dead body. The attitude of the disciples was that everything had finished in tragedy. (*The Gospel of Mark* [Philadelphia: Westminster Press, 1956], 387)

Contrast this despairing, defeated state of mind with the book of Acts. The same people who had no hope were abounding in hope. The same people who were afraid were suddenly faithful and fearless. The transformation is total and requires explanation.

Halford E. Luccock has a story that makes my point. He told of a man who was looking for the first time at "the stupendous spectacle" of the Grand Canyon. After a long period of silent awe the man said, "Something must have happened here." Then Luccock, with wry humor said, "It was a bit obvious. It was obvious that an Indian dragging a stick along the ground did not cause that deep cut in the earth. Such a result demanded an adequate cause" (*The Interpreter's Bible*, vol. 7 [New York: Abingdon Press, 1951], 913). How are we to explain the change in the people close to Jesus? How are we to explain the rise of the church? How are we to explain the energy required to cause Christianity to overcome the pagan religions that cluttered the Roman world?

People who have great difficulty believing the resurrection are driven to recognize that the people closest to Jesus must have believed. How else do we account for their transformation? I've gone to some length to describe the state of mind of the defeated followers of Jesus on Sunday morning. The part that requires more serious thought is the state of mind of those same people after they got the good news. Something must have happened here!

III. The Message of the Angel: Go and Tell!

"But he said to them, 'Do not be alarmed; you are looking for Jesus of Nazareth, who was crucified. He has been raised; he is not here. Look, there is the place they laid him. But go, tell his disciples and Peter that he is going ahead of you to Galilee; there you will see him, just as he told you' " (16:6-7). Every Easter this message needs to be broadcast to our cynical, jaded culture. Here is what the angel said to them and to us:

(1) "Do not be alarmed." Most of the time, when God spoke to people through an angel, the opening line was, "Do not be afraid" (see Lk 1:30). Anytime God comes close, we become afraid. Usually this fear is misplaced. Jesus told us that God is friendly, not frightening; we are slow to get the message.

(2) "You are looking for Jesus of Nazareth, who was crucified." There was no mistake. The women were not at the wrong tomb. The body had not been stolen. All identity problems are put down by this clear, almost legal definition of Jesus.

(3) "He has been raised; he is not here." Sometime before dawn on a Sunday morning, God had acted. The lifeless body of Jesus had become warm again. Life and breath came to him. As Peter said in his Pentecost sermon, "This Jesus God raised up, and of that all of us are witnesses" (Acts 2:32).

Sad to say, you can go to most churches for months and never hear a word about resurrection. Easter is the exception. Most Christian funerals will make some reference to it. But most of our "church talk" is about our personal problems, social issues, or life in our congregation. The early church trumpeted the resurrection. I looked into the eyes of some of the people who were up close to the World Trade Towers on 9/11. They had a faraway look in their eyes. They didn't know what to make of what had happened. A few spoke of God and hope; more were dazed, confused, and afraid. We all need to hear from that angel again.

(4) "But go, tell his disciples and Peter that he is going ahead of you to Galilee; there you will see him, just as he told you." Resurrection put the disciples in motion. They had been inert, passive. Easter morning energized them. Luccock said, "Good news simply cannot walk. It runs" (*The Interpreter's Bible*, vol. 7, 914). I've studied churches and preachers. The more seriously they take Jesus and resurrection, the more active they are. "Go and tell" still commands them. They are into missions. They attempt personal evangelism. They give their money and their children to Christ's service. They almost have marching orders.

This text is appropriate at every funeral. It needs to appear often in our church worship. Our children need to know Easter is not tacked on to our religion; it is at the center of it. God did not stand down and allow evil to triumph; the wickedness of Friday gave way to the goodness of Sunday. There is reason for hope. God and good are still in the contest. Angels are still speaking.